NIMROD

NIMROD
THE CENTENARIAN AIRCRAFT

BILL GUNSTON
OBE FRAeS

SPELLMOUNT

First published 2009

Spellmount Publishers
The History Press
The Mill, Brimscombe Port
Stroud, Gloucestershire, GL5 2QG
www.thehistorypress.co.uk

British Library Cataloguing in Publication Data.
A catalogue record for this book is available from the British Library.

ISBN 978-0-7524-5270-8

Typesetting and origination by The History Press
Printed in Great Britain

Contents

Acknowledgements

As will be explained in Chapter 8, it would have been a mere paragraph or two at the end of the preceding chapter had it not been for the diligent ferreting of Jon Lake. His research was first published in *Air International*, whose Editor I also thank. I also owe a considerable debt of gratitude to Ian Goold, who went to great lengths to point me towards useful sources. Of course, a particular feature of this book is the valuable inclusion of cutaways and other artwork, by Mike Badrocke (pp 112–113 and 150–151) and John Weal (pp 130–131). John's cutaway is included courtesy of Key Publishing. I am grateful to Mike Ramsden, former Editor in Chief of *Flight International*, for discovery of the empty weight of the Comet 1. I acknowledge the supply of photographs by Philip Birtles, Phil Jarrett, Paul Tomlin and Neville Beckett. Not least, I warmly appreciate the diligent attention to detail of everyone at Spellmount, especially Shaun Barrington and Max Hubbard. Obviously, any remaining glitches are down to the author.

Preface

In December 1942, at the height of the Second World War, the British Prime Minister, Winston Churchill, called in his Minister of Aircraft Production, Lord Brabazon, and suggested that something should be done to create new civil transport aircraft, to compete in the post-war world. This remarkable example of long-range vision resulted in several of Britain's largest aircraft companies beginning to work on purely civil airliners. One of these projects, called the Brabazon IV, was for an aircraft of a totally new type: a civil aircraft propelled by jet engines.

At this time the turbojet was a completely new and radical form of aircraft propulsion. It was also secret. Most British aircraft companies were so overworked that they were happy to leave challenging new technology to others, but an important exception was de Havilland Aircraft, at Hatfield, in Hertfordshire. Indeed, the de Havilland Engine Company, at Stag Lane and Stonegrove, in Edgware, Middlesex, had already designed a turbojet, and, in partnership with the project team at Hatfield, was eagerly studying various possible civil jet aircraft. Thus, the Brabazon IV proposal was assigned to de Havilland.

Eventually, this led to the world's first jet airliner, the D.H.106 Comet. Mindful that they were treading into the unknown, the de Havilland Aircraft team carried out exhaustive testing to make sure that there were no unknowns left uninvestigated, and that this trailblazing new aircraft was safe. In the spring of 1952, years ahead of other countries, it began flying fare-paying passengers on scheduled services, with the British national airline. Once the world's airlines had seen that this astonishing aircraft carried people and cargo in wonderful smoothness, twice as fast and twice as high as other transports, they queued to buy it.

Then, literally out of the blue, disaster struck. Comets suffered a succession of accidents, and even began mysteriously to disappear in flight. In January 1954, the aircraft that had flown the very first scheduled service somehow 'exploded' as it was climbing to high altitude. This triggered the most searching investigation into an aircraft accident there had ever been up to that point. Cutting a long story short, a totally redesigned and much more capable Comet at last entered service in 1958, but by that time there were larger, faster and longer-ranged rivals. Instead of perhaps 1,000, the last Comet was the 113th, and the future belonged to the competitors.

What nobody had expected was that in 1964, right at the end of Comet production, the same basic design would be selected as the basis for a long-range ocean-patrol and anti-submarine aircraft. In due course, this went into service with the Royal Air Force, named the Nimrod.

In conditions of great secrecy, a totally different Nimrod has established a reputation as the best intelligence-gathering aircraft in the world. Perhaps predictably, it is now likely to be partnered, and eventually replaced, by an American aircraft.

These established Nimrod versions could have been joined by a dramatically different development, a Nimrod-based AWACS (Airborne early-Warning and Control System). In typically British manner, in an acrimonious and deeply flawed environment, this version was rejected in favour of an American aircraft, which, though it was not designed to fly the British missions, appeared to British politicians and even high-ranking officers in the RAF, as obviously superior. British Aerospace was specifically instructed to destroy all the Nimrods of this version, to ensure that their development could not be continued.

This still left the Nimrod as the long-range oceanic aircraft, and today a totally upgraded multi-role version, the MRA.4, is about to enter service with the RAF. This too has been repeatedly threatened with cancellation, in order to save money. This is despite the fact that (again) no other aircraft can come near to fulfilling all the challenging tasks for which this aircraft has been designed. If by any miracle this should influence the British Treasury, the MRA.4, could well be in service through the 2040s.

Thus, the original D.H.106 design could become the first flying machine in history to sustain a continuous programme of development and use lasting for over 100 years. This is all the more surprising, in that this remarkable story is repeatedly punctuated by examples of how *not* to do it.

Chapter 1

A Jet Airliner

The story begins in late-1942, when two groups of British aeronautical engineers began to study something that had never been seriously considered previously: a jet-propelled transport aircraft. One group were members of a high-powered committee, which had been formed under the chairmanship of Lord Brabazon to consider what types of civil transport aircraft would be needed after the Second World War had been won. This committee had been set up in response to a suggestion made by the far-seeing Prime Minister. It first met on 23 December 1942, in the Council Room of the Royal Aeronautical Society, in central London.

At this time air travel in the United States was already a mass market, carrying thousands of every kind of passenger each day. In California, Douglas and Lockheed were producing modern transport aircraft, which, in the immediate post-war era, would grow into 100-seaters. In contrast, British air travel was largely confined to an exclusive group of senior officers and government messengers, and airliners were required only to carry such exalted people, and sacks of official mail. Thus, the Brabazon I project, regarded as the most immediately important, was for a long-range four-engined transport designed to carry just twelve passengers, in large armchairs, arranged four to a cabin. More speculative, the Brabazon IV was to be a mail carrier, with unprecedented speed conferred by having jet engines. This was assigned to the de Havilland Aircraft Co.

This company, based at Hatfield, Hertfordshire, was the other group which pioneered jet transport studies. It had made its name in the 1920s with simple light aircraft, notably the Moth biplane. However, from 1937 its design team, led by R. E. Bishop, boldly created such challenging projects as a graceful four-engined transport monoplane (the D.H.91 Albatross), a twin-engined monoplane transport of all metal stressed-skin construction (the D.H.95 Flamingo), a multi-role twin-engined aircraft of all wood construction yet faster than any RAF fighter (the D.H.98 Mosquito), and a jet-propelled fighter of radical design (the D.H.100 Vampire).

Even after the start of the Second World War, on 3 September 1939, the project staff at Hatfield kept drawing interesting concepts. In 1941, the Flamingo and Mosquito were both studied with axial turboprops. A year later Bishop and his team were sketching jet aircraft designed to carry mails, and even passengers. One of the most popular arrangements was to carry the payload in a short central nacelle, with the engines (two or three) at the back, with short jetpipes, and mount the tail on two booms projecting behind the wings. This layout was actually adopted for the D.H.100 fighter, dubbed the Spider Crab, and later officially named Vampire. An even more radical arrangement studied was to replace the horizontal tail by a foreplane, but Bishop recalled that 'nobody really liked this'.

By the time the de Havilland company was assigned the Brabazon IV project, in July or August 1943, the D.H.100 had completed a rapid and successful design period, and the first example began flight testing on 26 September. The author, aged 16, used to cycle 28 miles from his home in order to collect scrap balsa wood from Mosquito production, and will never forget an amazing event at the start of 1944. An extraordinary aircraft, camouflaged on top and yellow underneath, whistled over his head, to land like a bat on the runway. It was obviously jet-propelled.

Its engine was the D.H. Engine Company's H.1 Goblin turbojet, H standing for Chief Designer Maj. Frank Halford. This had a large single-sided centrifugal compressor, and, on test at Hatfield, was giving about 2,700 lb thrust, but aiming at 3,000 lb (1,361 kg). To minimise risk, the Brabazon IV was schemed as a D.H.100 scaled up to a span of 80 ft (24.4 m), with three closely spaced H.1 engines. However, it soon became obvious that such an aircraft would be deficient in range, or in payload, or both. Throughout 1944 the project team, led by C.T. Wilkins, reshaped the concept, and repeatedly enlarged it, in order to enhance its capability.

Gradually, the small mail carrier metamorphosed into a useful passenger carrier, though the cabin was still hardly larger than that of a DC-3.

The key question had originally been whether a jet aircraft could carry sacks of mail, almost all of it government or military, non-stop across the North Atlantic. By mid-1944 it was obvious that a more useful aircraft would instead carry up to twenty passengers, but this would mean reducing the range to not more than about 2,000 miles (3,219 km). This was the objective when, in late-1944, the national airline, British Overseas Airways Corporation (BOAC), made the startling announcement that it was interested in purchasing twenty-five of the world's first jet transport. At this time the airline was thinking in terms of an almost uselessly small aircraft; on 3 July 1945 it suggested 'a range of 700–800 miles, a cruising speed of over 450 mph … and a payload of 3,000 lb including 14 passengers'. Accordingly, the Ministry of Aircraft Production, which in the same month was merged into the Ministry of Supply (MoS), issued Specification 20/44. Now de Havilland had to deliver, calling the project the D.H.106, but the design was still fluid.

Even tailless configurations were still being considered, and when the wings were swept back these looked more attractive. These shapes were considered so important that, in spring 1945, just as the war in Europe was ending, the Ministry agreed to fund two research aircraft without a horizontal tail. The contract for two D.H.108 aircraft, based on Vampire fuselages, was placed in October of that year. Later a third was added. The Vampire was in production by English Electric, but the special D.H.108 fuselages were made at Hatfield. By November 1945 the first of these was mated with a dramatically different wing, with a leading-edge sweep of 43 degrees and trailing-edge elevons, able to control in both pitch and roll. This flew on 15 May 1946, by which time the second D.H.108, designed for higher speeds – possibly exceeding the speed of sound – was nearing completion. It had a different control system, and a wing with slats on a leading edge swept slightly more acutely, at 45 degrees, but by this time the D.H.106 had a horizontal tail, and the D.H.108 was no longer relevant.

Pressure for the D.H.106 to carry more, and thus do a useful job in a changing peacetime market, was relentless. Through 1945 the number of passenger seats rose from 20 to 28, 32 and eventually to 36, all on a level floor. This growth resulted in an increase in fuselage diameter, initially to 117 in (2,972 mm) and ultimately to 120 in (3,048 mm), and to repeated increases in fuselage length. These changes caused the project to become the Brabazon IVB. Having started with three and then four H.1 engines, the project now needed at least three of the larger H.2 engines, which started at 4,000 lb (1,814 kg) thrust and quickly grew to 5,000 lb (2,268 kg). This engine, soon named the Ghost, was already a firm programme, in order to power the D.H.112 Venom fighter. As this was derived from the Vampire, its Ghost engine featured diagonal air inlets, fed from the wing roots.

From late-1944 the D.H.106 propulsion had settled on not three but four of these engines, initially mounted close together under the fuselage. Here, it was thought that the engines might ingest material thrown up by the nosewheels. Accordingly, they were moved out under the wing roots. The simplest answer would have been to hang the engines directly under the wing, as was done in the Avro Ashton and Avro Canada Jetliner, but de Havilland sought a more elegant installation.

Finally, in early-1946, a novel arrangement emerged in which the left and right pairs of engines were actually inside the thickened root of each wing, between the main spars. In order to avoid having to redesign the engine, it was proposed to use curved ducts from inlets above and under the wing. This was really a non-starter, and eventually it was decided to bite the bullet and feed air from a single inlet in the leading edge of the wing, direct to a circular inlet on the engine. The jet-pipes were extended to end at the trailing edge. Such an arrangement would have been impossible with engines driving propellers. It was partly to reduce the root chord of the wing (distance from leading edge to trailing edge), making buried engines more attractive, that it was decided to fit a horizontal tail, and to reduce sweep-back from 40 degrees to a mere 20 degrees. This still made it difficult to achieve an elegant structure, and when one studies the two widely spaced spars, with various intermediate transverse bulkheads, the difficulty of the millions of stress calculations – without the benefit of computers, and with every digit written by hand in large books – is only too obvious. The virtual elimination of sweep-back also reduced the calculated cruising speed from 535 mph (861 km/h) to 505 mph (813 km/h). This was still more than 60 per cent faster than other airliners then being developed.

On 4 September 1946 the Minister of Supply placed a firm order for two D.H.106 prototype aircraft. The supposed BOAC 'order' for twenty-five back in 1944 was never a contractual document. The de Havilland management harboured no illusions regarding the magnitude of the task they were taking on. They enlisted the help of many specialist companies, such as Automotive Products (Lockheed, but not to be confused with the US company of the same name) and H. M. Hobson for hydraulics and powered flight controls; Aero Research (Ciba) for Redux metal bonding; S. Smith and Kelvin Hughes for flight-control systems and instruments; Lucas for engine and fuel controls; Rotax for electrical-power items; and Normalair for the cabin-air system. Many other suppliers appeared later.

The first contract for production aircraft, for eight for BOAC, was placed on 21 January 1947. Later in that year British South American Airways ordered an additional nine. By that time the aircraft had been named Comet, repeating the name of the D.H.88 racer of 1934. Throughout, the tightest possible secrecy was maintained, in the not unreasonable belief that what was being created had no parallel anywhere else in the world. Construction of the first Comet started in a secure hangar at Hatfield, de Havilland's public relations manager, Martin Sharp,

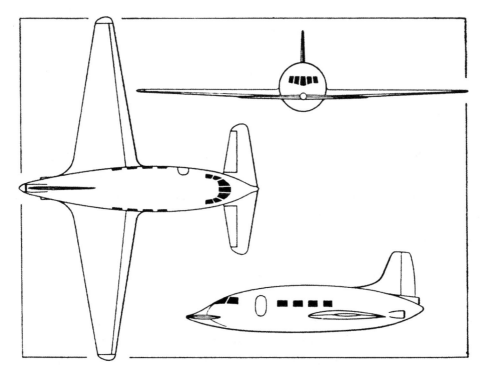

The earliest attempts to create jet transport were often totally unconventional. This de Havilland study of 1942 was a tail-first canard, designed mainly to carry mail. Three H.1 engines were grouped in the rear fuselage.

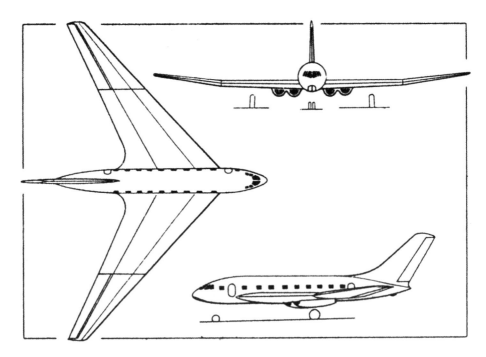

By January 1945 the early studies had begun to settle down as the D.H.106, which by this time was seen mainly as a passenger airliner. There was still no horizontal tail, but the four H.2 engines were now under the roots of the highly swept wing.

doing the reverse of his normal duties in trying to deflect interest being shown by the Press.

Meanwhile, everything possible was being done to ensure that the Comet, when it emerged, would be a reliable and safe vehicle. The fact that it would be roughly twice as fast as previous transports did not appear, by itself, to be a major problem. For flight control, a 'brute force and ignorance' philosophy saw de Havilland bring in Automotive Products to help design fully powered surfaces, driven by irreversible hydraulic units supplied by three completely separate systems. The idea was that safe flight should still be possible after any single major failure. Painstaking efforts were made to subject all the powered flight-control units and drive linkage to prolonged testing, because any failure could still have been serious.

To accommodate the exceptional quantity of fuel, ordinary tanks were eliminated, and the actual interior of the wing structure was sealed to form 'integral tankage'. This was then still a completely novel idea, and tank specimens were

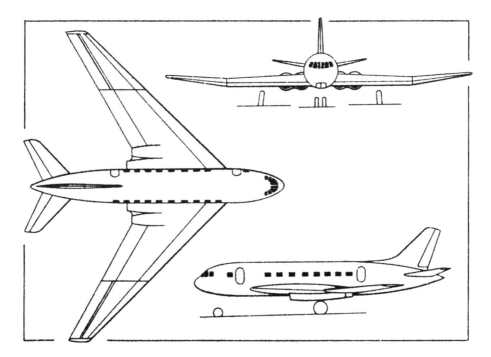

Steadily the D.H.106 grew a pressurised fuselage big enough to carry a useful number of passengers. By May 1946 the H.2 engines had been boldly placed actually inside the wing, and a horizontal tail had been added.

tested from 1946. Not least, the unprecedented cabin pressure made it necessary to subject such items as cabin windows to thousands of pressure reversals, using several times the intended design pressure.

In December 1947 Boeing rolled out the first XB-47, later named the Stratojet. This was a startling strategic bomber, with six turbojets hung externally under an amazingly slender wing, swept back at 35 degrees. Nobody had seen anything like it. When I became a staff man on *Flight,* I wrote a major treatise analysing the pros and cons of the two kinds of engine installation, inside the wing or on pylons beneath it. This article generated passionate interest, and 'buried engines' became a national trademark adopted on the three types of V-bomber for the RAF. Despite that, I think the final answer is that today's Nimrod is, in terms of engine installation, a dinosaur. That still does not mean that it suffers any loss in either speed or range, compared with engines hung externally. Aircraft design is not immune to mere fashion.

Chapter 2

The Comet 1

By the start of 1948, the first two Comets were taking shape at Hatfield. Built on Ministry of Supply account, and regarded as prototypes, they bore Construction Numbers 06001 and 06002, and differed in several respects from the production Comet I for BOAC. The most obvious difference was that, late in the design stage, it had been decided to use a completely redesigned main landing gear. Also, small rocket engines were externally visible, permanently installed to give extra thrust for take-off from hot or high-altitude airports.

Originally, when the D.H.106 was still a small mailplane, it had seemed logical to use not only a wing scaled up aerodynamically from that of the Vampire or D.H.108, but also an enlarged form of the same main landing gear, with a single wheel on a leg that retracted outwards into the wing. By the time the first two aircraft were being built, the take-off weight had escalated to about 50 tons, and the main landing gears had accordingly become clumsy and unattractive. Under each wing was an enormous single wheel, retracting outwards, the bay being closed by large doors. The retracted gears caused unsightly bulges.

In 1938 Douglas had adopted a similar arrangement on the original DC-4, but for the production derivative changed to neat twin-wheel units. For the production Comet, de Havilland went a stage further, and in partnership with Lockheed (Automotive Products), designed a pioneer four-wheel bogie. This had a single large shock strut, which, via an upper rocker arm, reacted the loads from front and rear pivoted arms carrying the axles. Major components were forged in Hiduminium R.R.77 light alloy. On the axles were inboard and outboard pairs of wheels, with quite small 36 × 10 − 18 tyres, inflated to what was then the high pressure of 150 lb/sq in (10.5 kg/cm²). The powerful multi-disc brakes on all four wheels were controlled by the newly invented Dunlop Maxaret system, which prevented any locking of the wheels during harsh braking, even on ice or snow. The nose gear had two unbraked wheels, with 30 × 9 − 15 tubeless tyres, retracting to the rear. It could be hydraulically steered over ±59°, and for towing on the ground, after attaching a warning pennant, the steering link could be

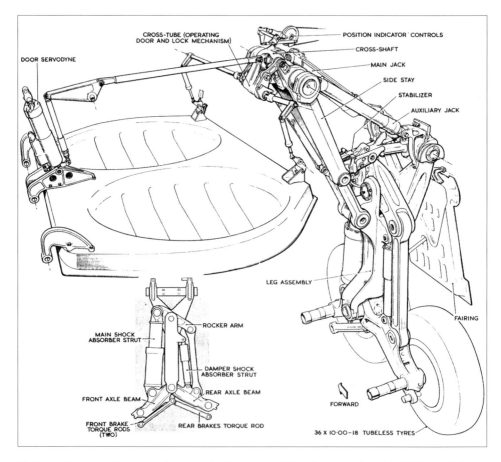

This drawing actually shows the main landing gear of the Comet 4, but this differs only in small details from that of all other production Comets. Indeed, even the main gears of the Nimrod MRA.4 are in principle exactly the same.

disconnected. This enabled the aircraft to be rotated on a vertical axis without moving forward.

In its basic shape, the Comet was conventional, at least in comparison with the tailless canard projects, and the remaining sweep-back of the wing was little more than leading-edge taper. Surprisingly, one of the few external features that did concern the designers was the almost perfectly streamlined nose. This was expected to be fine in cruising flight, but several aerodynamicists considered that, when approaching to land in heavy rain, the pilots might be blinded by a film of water. It was thought necessary to investigate this possibility before the first Comet was built, and a wooden mock-up Comet nose was tested on an Airspeed Horsa glider, which had the same fuselage diameter. Towed by a Halifax, flown by 'Dizzie' de Villiers of the de Havilland Engine Company, through the worst weather that could be found, the only problem was the sick-making ride (it was in a Horsa that the author came nearest to disgracing himself).

Structurally, there were more serious problems, not least of which was that the fuselage would have to withstand an internal pressure differential of 8¼ lb/sq in (0.58 kg/cm²), roughly double that in any previous airliner. The ruling materials were the usual aluminium-based light alloys, and the enormously increased hoop stresses imposed by the unprecedented pressurisation could be withstood in two ways. One was simply to use thicker, and thus heavier, gauges of material. The designers were already fighting a battle against weight increase that was more difficult than usual, because of the need to carry an exceptional mass of fuel. Accordingly, it was decided to take the risky course of using normal – and in places even less than normal – skin thicknesses, and to rely on exceptionally complete testing of various specimens of the structure. These specimens included sections of fuselage, which were designed to a factor of 2.5, or 20.5 lb/in² (1.44 kg/cm²), and tested to a factor of 2, or 16.5 lb/in² (1.15 kg/cm²). The passenger windows were designed to a factor of 10, but a striking feature of the Comet was that these windows were square, like those in most unpressurised aircraft.

As a basic flying machine, the Comet was broadly conventional. The wings were aerodynamically not unusual, the ruling thickness/chord ratio being 11 per cent, though the root chord of almost 30 ft (9 m) was exceptional. Because of its streamlined shape and large mass, the Comet was also one of the first aircraft, apart from dive bombers, to be fitted with airbrakes. These took the form of narrow perforated strips, one hinged above and the other hinged under the wing, immediately ahead of the outboard flaps. The flaps themselves, though large, were surprisingly simple surfaces, hinged down by hydraulic jacks. Plain sections were fitted inboard and outboard beyond the engines, and there were split flaps under the jetpipes. As originally built, the first prototype was also fitted with automatic slats on the leading edge of the outer half of each wing.

Structurally, the wings, like the rest of the airframe, made unprecedented use of Redux bonding. This was a method of fastening metal parts together with adhesive. It had been developed by Dr N.A. de Bruyne at Aero Research, at Duxford, and was marketed by the Anglo-Swiss company Ciba. Initially test-flown on the Aero Research Snark of 1934, it was eagerly adopted by de Havilland, initially on the D.H.103 Hornet and D.H.104 Dove. Different grades were eventually marketed in the form of sheet, liquid or powder, the metal parts being bonded together under heat and pressure. As any perfora-

One of the few photographs showing the first Comet fitted with slats. *(Philip Jarrett)*

tions in a structure, such as holes drilled for rivets, are a potential source of weakness, it is clearly an advantage if parts can be merely stuck together. In the Comet, Redux was used extensively, for example, to bond stringers to the skin throughout the airframe. Reducing the number of rivet holes also made it easier to seal the wings for fuel. Unfortunately, to save time, some of the most critical structure, including some already Reduxed, was additionally riveted, as related later.

One area where there was much argument concerned the crucial problem of flight control. Eventually, this pioneer large multi-engine jet aircraft appeared to be so challenging that it was decided to make the flight-control surfaces fully powered. Aerodynamically, however, they were quite conventional, comprising large ailerons, elevators and a one-piece rudder. Each surface was driven by a pivoted linkage from a Lockheed Servodyne power unit, in a duplicated (primary and secondary) hydraulic system of pipes and valves which, in the D.H.106 prototypes, was originally filled with traditional mineral oil to specification DTD.585. The production Comets introduced supposedly non-inflammable Skydrol, made by Monsanto to specification DTD.900/4081. Whereas wartime aircraft had typically used a system pressure of 1,000 lb/sq in (70 kg/cm^2), the Comet's hydraulic systems operated to a ruling pressure of 2,500 lb/sq in (176 kg/cm^2). They operated not only the flight controls, but also the flaps, airbrakes, landing-gear retraction, wheel brakes and nosewheel steering.

Each hydraulic system was identified by a colour. The Green system, energised by Mk 7 pumps on engines 2 (left inner) and 4 (right outer), provided normal operation of the landing gear, main-gear doors, wheel brakes, steering, airbrakes and flaps. In the case of Blue failure, Green could also operate the flight-control surfaces, via the secondary Servodynes. Blue provided for normal operation of the flight controls, via the primary Servodynes. Yellow came into play only following failure of both Green and Blue, to provide power to the secondary Servodynes. Red provided for emergency extension of the landing gears, and, following Green failure, for emergency operation of items normally driven by that system. Red also supplied sustained pressure to the wheel brakes, for parking, and for ground testing of Green services. As a last resort, following multiple failures, a hatch in the floor of the flight deck provided access to a hand pump. This pump was also available for topping up fluid levels.

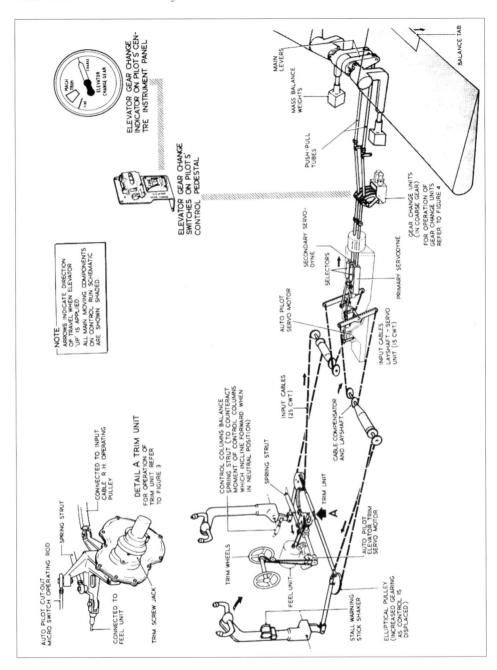

In designing the Comet almost every functioning system broke new ground, and in many cases was totally unlike anything seen previously. Nowhere was this more true than with the flight-control system. Shown here is the control circuit for the elevators, with the captain's yoke commanding a climb.

Though it did not involve so much completely new technology, the electrical system was just as unprecedented. Whereas the D.H.89 Dragon Rapide had had fourteen electrical items, including plugs and fuzes, and a typical D.H.98 Mosquito around 300, in the Comet the number exceeded 10,000. Moreover, all these items had to work at a cruising altitude of up to 40,000 ft (12 km). The basic power supply came from two busbars, with current return through the airframe structure. Raw power was generated by a Rotax three-phase alternator on each engine, rated at 14 kVA, or about 20 hp. With the aircraft parked, power was supplied by six 24-V batteries, which could be connected in series to provide 120-V power to start the No 2 engine. This engine could then supply power to start the others. The electrical bay was under the floor, behind the nose gear. External-power sockets were provided for 120-V a.c., 112-V d.c. and the traditional 28-V d.c.

The Comet was one of the first British aircraft to have a high-power a.c. system, and it also used almost wholly electrical instrumentation. As will be explained later, all had a version of the Smiths SEP.2 autopilot, and production aircraft were fitted with a pioneer weather radar, usually supplied by E. K. Cole (Ekco), in the nose. Sensors throughout the aircraft could warn the crew of failures, and emergency action in the event of fire was managed electrically.

At the start there was no argument regarding the engine. The de Havilland H.2 Ghost was already being developed for the D.H.112 fighter, which became the Venom, and at first the same engine appeared suitable for the wing-root installation, with inlets above and below the wing. As noted earlier, this unique arrangement was eventually changed to a long duct from the leading edge to a single circular inlet on the engine. With a mass flow of up to 87 lb (39.5 kg) of air per second, the Comet's Ghost 50 was considered very powerful, but today's GE90–115B, with an airflow of 3,618 lb (1,641 kg) per second, would not fit inside the Comet's fuselage. Priority was naturally given to the engine for the Venom, but the first Ghost 50 went on test on 2 September 1945. Eventually two Avro Lancastrians had their outboard Merlins replaced by Ghost 50 engines, fed with kerosene from separate tankage, and the first began flight testing on 24 July 1947.

When the D.H.106 was just a project, many performance engineers were concerned that, as there would be no helpful slipstream blowing back across the wing from propellers, the take-off run might be very long, especially at hot or high-altitude airports. At that time the standard method of boosting the take-off acceleration was to use jettisonable solid-propellant rocket motors, commonly known as Jato (jet-assisted take-off). Instead of this simple method, the de Havilland Engine Co. produced a specially designed reusable rocket engine. Named the Sprite, it was a self-contained package comprising a refillable tank of HTP (high-test hydrogen peroxide) fed by bottled compressed air to a simple rocket chamber. When filled, it weighed 950 lb (431 kg). Mounted in the trailing edge of each wing, between the main-engine jetpipes, each Sprite added 5,000 lb (2,268 kg) of thrust, until the tank ran dry after some eleven seconds. Tested on the first Comet, it was already obvious that airlines would be reluctant to accept such dangerous material as HTP, and the idea of booster rockets was quickly abandoned.

One of the major decisions was to install the engines inside a specially thickened inboard section of each wing. On each side of the aircraft centreline, Rib 1 was alongside the pressurised tubular fuselage. Immediately outboard were the Nos 2 and 3 engines, each in a supposedly fireproof bay, Zone 1 being ahead of the engine's turbine and Zone 2 behind. Outboard of Rib 2 were engines 1 and 4. The slightly back-swept wing spars were pierced by large holes, through which passed the engine air-inlet duct or the jetpipe. Small NACA-type flush inlets fed ventilation air through each engine bay, and Zone 2 was additionally ventilated by a small ram inlet above the engine, and a second above the jetpipe. The jetpipes pointed directly to the rear, but in later Comets they were angled outward, and also extended, to reduce acoustic damage to the fuselage. The installation is installed on page 45.

The first Comet, with company Construction No. 06001, was fitted with the first flight-cleared Ghost 50 engines, rated at 4,450 lb (19.8 kN) at 10,250 rpm. Initial production Mk I Comets had similar engines fully rated at 5,000 lb (22.24 kN), and the Comet IA, described later, had engines cleared to 5,050 lb (22.46 kN) dry, and 5,600 lb (24.91 kN) with water injection. Spraying demineralised water into the compressor or the combustion chambers cooled the incoming air, increasing its density so that more fuel could be injected. Starting was electric, the Rotax C.5901 motor driving directly on the front of the mainshaft. Each engine had an integral oil tank, which in production Comets was filled with synthetic Esso Aviation Turbo Oil 35. The oil coolers were between each pair of engines, fed by an oval ram-air inlet in the wing leading edge.

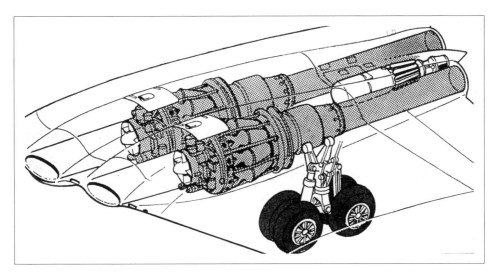

On the first Comet, to boost thrust on take-off, a de Havilland Sprite rocket engine was installed between each pair of Ghost main engines. From front to rear each Sprite package comprised the tank of HTP, the eight bottles of high-pressure air, and the thrust chamber and nozzle. This drawing also highlights the length of duct needed to feed air to each main engine, and to join the engine to the final nozzle.

The first Comet, G-ALVG, is seen here on its first take-off after being fitted with Super Sprite rocket engines. *(Philip Birtles)*

As already noted, the Comet was one of the first aircraft to have a large fuel capacity entirely of the 'integral' type, in which the aircraft structure itself contains the fuel, with no separate tanks. In the Comet I there were nine tanks, one under the cabin floor and four in each wing. Each was provided with an access panel in the underside secured by removable set-screws, so that, during a major overhaul, the interior could be inspected. Total capacity was almost exactly 6,050 Imp. gal. (27,503 litres, 7,266 US gal.) and in an emergency almost all of it could be jettisoned through a pipe at the kink in the trailing edge of each wing. Each pipe incorporated a flexible section, so that it could hinge down when the flap above it was lowered.

The system posed many challenges, and its new features are worth recording. To load such a large quantity of fuel as quickly as possible, novel self-sealing couplings were provided in the underside of the outer wing tanks, to which a pressure-fuelling hose socket could be inserted and screwed in tightly. By this means the fuel could be put on board much faster than by putting a nozzle loosely into a traditional over-wing filler. The author wrote an account of this, entitled '20 tons in 20 minutes'. Each tank incorporated an electrical-capacitance sensor, which, unlike previous measuring devices, such as pivoted floats, could give an accurate reading even if the aircraft should somehow become inverted. Another clever feature was a 'dripstick' in the inboard underside of each tank. This was a vertical graduated telescopic tube, which could be unscrewed and carefully pulled down. The moment fuel began to run out, the tank contents could be read off the stick.

In the August 1949 issue of the excellent *de Havilland Gazette* the chief power-plant engineer, John E. Walker, wrote the first detailed account of such tankage. He did not relate it to the Comet, but the connection was obvious. On 24 April 1952 the author went to Luton, to hear Walker deliver the first detailed account of the Comet's tankage and fuel system, in a Royal Aeronautical Society lecture.

This was the first time any specific details of the Comet had escaped into the public domain. Even after the Comet was in regular service, de Havilland still refused to let any journalist have any details whatsoever, and specifically instructed airline customers to keep their Comet technical manuals under lock and key. To try to steal a march on us, *The Aeroplane*, published a pseudo cutaway, drawn with a stick of charcoal by Leslie Carr, who was an artist but not a technical artist.

Not until *Flight*'s great Commercial Aircraft issue of 6 July 1956 did a detailed drawing appear publicly, and the same issue also contained the first cutaways of the much more capable 707 and DC-8.

Another system posing unprecedented problems was the pressurisation and air conditioning. Not only did this operate at a very high pressure-differential, but it also was the first in Britain, and second in the world, to add water vapour to keep humidity at a comfortable 30 per cent. Today, many pressurised aircraft lack such a feature, and this can result in passengers suffering from sore throats. On the other hand, modern systems do not bleed air from the engines. There is always a risk of contamination from lubricant or fuel, and modern systems use the hot bleed to heat fresh air, whereas in the Comet the fresh air rammed in through small inlets in the wing leading edge was used to cool the bleed air on its way to the cabin. If necessary, further cooling could be provided by a CAU (cold-air unit). This was a small high-speed turbine, rather like a miniature turbojet operating in reverse. It was a product of Sir George Godfrey & Partners, the principal subcontractor on the main system being Normalair, a subsidiary of Westland Aircraft.

The filtered and conditioned air was piped in from each wing, to a large pack under the cabin floor. From here most of the flow was ducted up two conduits which curved round the fuselage wall, inside the main cabin bulkhead above the front spar, to the ceiling. Ducts then carried it along the length of the cabin, and thence down the wall, inside the trim, to numerous outlets at floor level. Special supplies warmed the feet of the pilots, and demisted the cockpit windows. Most of the flow was recycled along ducts immediately below the supply channel in the roof, covered by perforated vinyl trim. Used air finally escaped in a controlled manner, through a one-way pressurisation pack under the floor of the rear fuselage, with an auxiliary pack further forward in case of failure of the discharge valves under the fuselage. Should the aircraft have to ditch, these one-way valves could be screwed down manually.

At the Comet's unprecedented cruising height, the atmosphere was so cold and dry that icing was impossible, but protection was still necessary as the aircraft climbed or descended through the lower atmosphere. Under the nose were arranged left and right ice detectors. These were simple T-shaped pipes, with a forward-facing aperture (in effect, a pitot tube), and a smaller one facing aft. Thus, the detectors normally sensed a positive pressure, but if the pitot tube became blocked by ice, the situation suddenly changed. The positive pressure vanished, and the aft-facing tube sucked air out of an aneroid capsule. This contracted, triggering the de-icing system. A small electric motor would then start rotating, but with the drive clutch disengaged. Simultaneously, current would start heating the blocked ice detector, and a warning light would appear in the cockpit. As soon as the detector head was clear of ice, the capsule would return to normal, allowing the motor clutch to engage and drive a camshaft controlling the regular de-icing cycle, the warning light remaining on. Hot compressor bleed air was used directly to de-ice the engine inlets, and the double-skin leading edges of the wings, tailplane and rudder. Transparent Triplex GF (gold film), then a new invention, could electrically heat the cockpit windows.

It is appropriate to conclude this description of the Comet I by reviewing the avionics and emergency equipment, though the two prototypes lacked many items, and in any case carried a considerable amount of special flight-test instrumentation. The principal radio for use over routes where, in the mid-20th Century, aeronautical radio stations were many hundreds of miles apart, was the Marconi AD.307/AD.118. This was a traditional h.f. (high-frequency) set, served by two antenna (aerial) wires which ran from points above the mid-fuselage to connections on the leading edge of the fin. The AD.307 was provided with another new device, Selcal, a selective-calling system which automatically permitted ground stations to send messages to a particular aircraft, unheard by any other.

In the author's opinion, h.f. suffered from static interference, and speech distortion, while the clearer shorter wavelengths lacked the necessary range. Over shorter ranges v.h.f. was much better, the Comet I having the Marconi AD.304/AD.704, provided in duplicate, with manual tuning by the radio operator over 360 channels; later Comets had precise crystal selection. The v.h.f. antenna for the No.1 set was in the top of the fin, the whole local structure being dielectrically insulated. The v.h.f. No.2 was served by an aft-facing blade antenna under the fuselage, in line with the wing leading edge.

The h.f. wire antennas also served APN-9, the Loran (long-range navigation) set. This was a navigation aid developed by the United States during the Second World War, based on pulses continuously emitted by special ground stations. Other navaids included twin ADF (automatic direction finding) sets, the Marconi

AD.712 being selected. Their sense antennas, necessary to avoid a possible error of 180 degrees, were two prominent parallel rails, like handrails, along the underside of the centre fuselage. The vital fixed loop antennas were recessed into the top of the fuselage, side-by-side behind the flight deck. Of course, the metal skin over these had to be cut away, and how this was done was to play a crucial part in the Comet's subsequent history. The ADF provided a continuous flight-deck reading of the aircraft's heading (course), and its bearing from two selected ground stations, and thus provided a fix.

A slightly later navaid was V.O.R., v.h.f. omni-range. This enabled the aircraft to navigate by flying from overhead each V.O.R. station to the next. It was to avoid the need to follow such ridiculous dog-legging tracks, often crowded with other traffic, that the British company Decca developed its obviously superior hyperbolic system, which enabled each aircraft to navigate individually along the shortest route. As this was not American, it was thrown out in a manner that can fairly be called scandalous, at a crucial series of ICAO (International Civil Aviation Organisation) meetings in 1957–59. Amazingly, V.O.R. is still in use.

All the navaid readouts, and many other items, were grouped at the station for the navigator, on the right-hand wall of the flight deck behind the co-pilot. For landings in bad weather, the universally adopted I.L.S. (instrument landing system) was fitted to production Comets, in duplicate. The I.L.S. glide-path antenna was in the nose, close to the radar, while the marker antenna, which indicated to the pilot progress along the glide-path, was flush with the under-skin of the fuselage, beside the left A.D.F. rail. Further aft, on the vertical centreline, was the omni (all-directions) antenna for the D.M.E. (distance-measuring equipment). This did what it said, reading out the distances to ground stations, which were usually co-located with the next V.O.R. The D.M.E. transmitting antenna was a small blade under the nose, whilst the homing antennas were on each side of the nose, ahead of the windscreens.

Standard equipment on most Comets was the Smiths SEP.2 autopilot system. This duplicated installation provided flight control about all three axes, including heading information, and radio-beam displacement for making semi-automatic landing approaches down an I.L.S. beam. It was not sufficiently precise for blind landing, which came much later. In production aircraft, the complete Smiths Flight System also served other functions, such as stabilising the scanner platform of the Ekco weather radar.

Smart retraction of the unusual landing gears on one of the first take-offs by G-5-1.
(Philip Jarrett)

G-ALVG is seen here in its original unpainted finish, after being fitted with the four-wheel bogie landing gears intended for production aircraft. On 'VG they could not be retracted. *(Philip Birtles)*

Even the prototypes naturally carried a comprehensive gaseous-oxygen system for use in the event of a serious loss of cabin pressure. Crew oxygen was supplied from two 2,250-litre high-pressure bottles, under the floor ahead of the wing. Production aircraft carried passenger oxygen in an adjacent bay, which held two bottles of 2,250 litres and one of 1,400. Following loss of cabin pressure, masks dropped down automatically at each seat, while the captain opened the airbrakes and lost height as rapidly as possible.

Like other British aircraft at the time, emergency equipment included Graviner Firewire throughout the under-floor area, and around the engines. Designed to indicate any abnormally high temperature, Firewire comprised a stainless steel capillary tube filled with insulating material, which prevented a fine wire down the centre from touching the wall. The insulator was a material whose electrical resistance fell sharply if it was heated. At a critical temperature, well above any reached in normal use, resistance fell to the point where current passed, and an alarm was sounded. Firewire remained active even if it should at some point be severed. Armed with the knowledge of where the fire was, the crew could then operate extinguishers located in critical areas, and take whatever other action was needed. Other detectors warned of light-obstructing matter, such as smoke, in the under-floor areas.

Emergency equipment also included life jackets stowed under the passenger seats, and, in production aircraft, four inflatable life-rafts, also known as dinghies. These were the RFD type 20UL, each for 20 persons, two of which were stowed in the root of each wing. Ditching the aircraft would automatically blow off the upper-skin covers, to release all four rafts. These would inflate rapidly, whilst still secured under two passenger windows on each side, which could be pulled open inwards. The flight crew could escape via a cockpit rope, thrown out on the right side.

At last, the first Comet, unpainted except for the Society of British Aircraft Constructors (SBAC) test registration G-5-1, was rolled out on 25 July 1949. Two days later, on 27 July, Chief Test Pilot John Cunningham began increasingly fast taxi testing, up and down the Hatfield runway, soon including brief hops. It happened to be his birthday, and also that of Sir Geoffrey de Havilland. After careful checks, John led his crew back on board: co-pilot John Wilson, flight engineer Frank Reynolds, observer Tony Fairbrother, and Harold Waters managing the complex electrics and instrumentation. At 6.17 p.m. G-5-1 began a flight-testing programme, that was to be remarkable for its absence of nasty surprises.

At the very start, the main problem was that, having been at Hatfield all day waiting for the big news, London's aviation Press corps, which then numbered over fifty, were sent away, shortly before the first take-off. One famous scribe said: 'I'll never visit de Havilland again!', and he never did.

Chapter 3

Disaster

Comet flight-testing went remarkably well, considering that this aircraft broke new ground in so many areas. One of the first modifications was to remove the slats, with almost no effect on handling. The author wondered if this might have been a mistake, as will be explored later. After painting on civil registration, G-ALVG, the first Comet, began to make headlines by setting records on overseas flights. Later it was given a white top to the fuselage, in keeping with current fashion, and the proud letters BOAC and the airline's Speedbird symbols, even though it actually belonged to the Ministry of Supply.

On 12 December 1949, the Minister himself, George Strauss, told Parliament that the total cost of the Comet programme to his Department so far, had been 'about £4 million', most of which was down to the Ghost engine. Nobody enquired whether this paid for development of the Ghost fighter version. The figure included the cost of the two Comet prototypes, and also the three D.H.108s.

On 27 July 1950, precisely a year after the start of flight testing, 'VG was joined by the second prototype, 'ZK. This approached closer to the production standard, apart from the interior furnishing, but it still had the single-wheel main landing gears. By this time, however, 'VG had been retrofitted with the bogie landing gears, although, to avoid a time-consuming rebuild of the wing, these had to remain permanently extended. Again, there were no serious problems.

A rare posed group of Hatfield flight-test personnel, gathered with the first Comet in the early 1950s. The wing is engaged in slat testing, and is fitted with a dummy Comet 3 pinion tank. *(Philip Birtles)*

G-ALZK, the second prototype, at Rome Ciampino (note man with chocks). *(Philip Jarrett)*

True production landing gears, able to retract, were first seen on 06003, registration 'YP, phonetically then rendered as Yoke Peter. This was the first of the eight Comet I aircraft for BOAC, which were announced as having cost £450,000 each. First flown on 9 May 1951, 'YP was fully furnished, and virtually identical to the Mk I aircraft that followed it. A month earlier, on 2 April, BOAC had opened a Comet Unit at Hurn, near Bournemouth, to carry out crew training and route proving.

On 2 May 1952, carrying a full load of thirty-six fare-paying passengers, and commanded by Capt. A. M. A. Majendie, 'Yoke Peter' flew the world's first scheduled jet service. The destination was Johannesburg, with refuelling stops at Rome, Beirut, Khartoum, Entebbe and Livingstone.

By this time American plane-makers, especially Boeing, Douglas and Lockheed, were beginning to be concerned. Publicly, their attitude was 'Heck, the Comet is useless, it has only thirty-six seats, burns fuel like crazy, and nobody could make money with it!' In fact, once they had seen the Comet's unprecedented passenger appeal, they realised that the future for vehicles that ploughed through a bumpy atmosphere, with intrusive cabin noise and vibration, and for twice as long, was going to be much shorter than had been expected. Lockheed spent nearly a million dollars building the L-1649 Starliner, with a new wing, and sold just forty-three.

In any case, de Havilland recognised that they could not rest on their laurels. From 1948 the design engineers at Hatfield had worked to improve the Comet, and make it carry more, with greater efficiency. The immediate upgrade was the Comet IA, after 1952 called the 1A, with the switch to Arabic numerals. The principal improvement was the modification of the Ghost 50 to give increased thrust for taking off from hot and high-altitude airports, by using methanol/water injection, as noted previously. It was also decided to angle the jetpipes slightly outward, to reduce noise and buffet impacting on the rear fuselage, and increase fuel capacity.

For the longer term, a much greater advance was to change to a different engine entirely. After sometimes difficult meetings with the de Havilland Engine Company, and with Rolls-Royce, the decision was taken to switch to the latter company's Avon, to power an aircraft to be designated Comet 2. In 1949 aircraft '06, 'YT, was switched to Ministry charge (it was replaced for BOAC by '012), set aside at Hatfield, and converted to take Avon engines as the Comet 2X. Distinguished by visibly enlarged engine inlets, it began its flight-test programme on 16 February 1952.

The Comet 2X, the sixth Comet, originally bore no markings except registration G-ALYT. Powered by Avon 500-series engines, it first flew on 16 February 1952, before the Comet 1 had entered BOAC service. Fitted with more mature Avon 502s, 'YT was delivered to BOAC for engine maturity and crew training on 29 June 1956. *(Philip Jarrett)*

The Avon was Rolls-Royce's first turbojet with an axial compressor, and its early years could hardly have been more discouraging. After switching to a two-stage turbine, and redesigning the compressor and several other parts, the RA.3 thrust rating of 6,500 lb (2,948 kg) was finally cleared in 1950, for the Canberra bomber. The civil Mk 501, at the same rating, was certificated soon afterwards. Compared with the Ghost, it was slightly heavier, at 2,520 lb (1,143 kg), but gave significantly higher take-off thrust and was more economical in use of fuel. In any case, Rolls-Royce was already testing later Avons, after an almost complete redesign, and these were to make possible the Comet's future development.

Though totally different from the Ghost, the Avon 501 fitted neatly inside the Comet 2 wing, and apart from the enlarged inlet and jet-pipe, changes in the installation were minor. The principal modification to the airframe was that the fuselage was extended by two bays, increasing length from 93 ft (28 m) to 96 ft (29 m), and enabling standard seating to be increased from thirty-six to forty-four. The passenger windows remained square.

Meanwhile, production built up rapidly at Hatfield, as orders from foreign customers began to flood in. To meet the demand, de Havilland arranged to build Comet 2s at the enormous factory at Broughton, near Chester. During the war, this had been known as RAF Hawarden (pronounced 'harden'), and had built 5,540 Wellington bombers. Shortly afterwards Short & Harland, at Belfast, were added to the Comet 2 production team. At Hatfield the immediate task was to complete the crucial Comet 1 order for BOAC. This now totalled nine aircraft, one of which had originally been the first of the nine ordered by BSAA, before that airline was forcibly merged into BOAC, the other eight going to other customers. Then production was to switch to the Mk 1A. The first of these, '013, G-ANAV, was retained by de Havilland. It began flight testing on 11 August 1952, six months later than the Avon-engined Mk 2X. It was followed by production Mk 1A Comets for Canadian Pacific, the French airlines UAT and Air France, and the Royal Canadian Air Force.

Beyond these, by mid-1952, fourteen other airlines were – most of them secretively – talking to de Havilland about the timing of future Comet developments. By this time de Havilland could feel that the world's first jet airliner was a proven product. There was just a nagging concern about the exceptionally high differential pressure (dP) in the fuselage, so in October 1952 a section of fuselage was placed in a water tank, and subjected to 10,000 cycles up to 1.25 times the design dP, or 10.3 lb/in². Water was used instead of air so that, should a failure occur, the test specimen should merely crack, rather than explode. In June 1953 it was decided to continue to 15,000 reversals.

Everything seemed to be going well when, on 26 October 1952, 'YZ crashed on take-off from Rome's Ciampino airport. It had simply failed to become airborne, and carried on thundering off the far end of the runway. At this point, Capt. R.E. 'Bob' Foote shut down power and braked hard, but it was too late. Fortunately, the ground was soft and level, and, despite gross fuel spillage, there was no fire. Everyone on board escaped with a severe shaking, but 'YZ was a write-off. As it was on Italian territory, the accident investigation was Italian, but with representatives from the British Accidents Investigation Branch (AIB) and de Havilland. Perhaps inevitably, the blame was placed on Foote, who took up a new career breeding poultry. He was found to have maintained 'an excessive

06021, registered F-BGNY as the second Comet 1A for Air France, on test from Hatfield on 12 June 1953. Delivered on 7 July, it was later returned to the UK, and used for BOAC crew training at Hurn before going to Boscombe Down. The fuselage is at the D.H. Heritage Museum. See photograph on page 52. *(Philip Jarrett)*

nose-up attitude' on take-off, but the chief ARB observer, Bob Nelson, privately considered that Foote had been blamed unfairly.

Today, the idea on take-off is to accelerate to a particular safe speed, called V_1, and then – and only then – to raise the nose so that the aircraft becomes airborne. Later a 'rotate' speed, typically $1.1V_1$, was added. With hindsight, Foote erred in rotating much too soon, quickly reaching a point where drag equalled the available thrust, with the wheels still firmly on the ground. At Hatfield, John Cunningham made dozens of nose-high runs down the runway, scraping the tail bumper. Clearly this was no way to become airborne, and wording was discussed for adding to the pilot's documentation, in capitals and underlined. The author asked Bishop 'Surely it was a mistake to do away with the slats?' After a pause, the design director replied 'I hope not.'

On 11 December 1952 the French airline UAT took delivery of the first Comet 1A to be sold, and the first Comet to be exported, 06015, F-BGSA. Cunningham set the pattern, in personally converting flight crews and, among other things, now emphasising the correct take-off procedure.

The next export customer was Canadian Pacific, whose first 1A, 06014, CF–CUN, *Empress of Australia*, was loaded to maximum weight with spare parts, documents and fuel, and departed on its long delivery flight on 1 March 1953. It was bound for Sydney, where it was to begin CPAL's trans-Pacific service. Capt. Charles Pentland and crew had been fully briefed on the safe take-off procedure, but at Karachi, in pitch darkness at 03.00 on 2 March, Pentland was defeated by his inability to see the horizon. He raised the nose far too early, realised what he was doing too late, slammed the nosewheels back on the runway, and proceeded off the airport. The Comet hit an open drainage culvert and burst into flames. All on board were killed. CPAL did not take delivery of No.12, which was to have been CF–CUM; instead, it became G–ANAV of BOAC to replace the Comet lost at Rome.

The inevitable inference was that, despite the deadly danger, and the careful schooling of Cunningham and his colleagues, customer pilots were going to keep raising the nose too early. The author again wondered whether removal of the slats had been a serious mistake. Bishop decided that the answer was to redesign the wing leading edge with what at that time was popularly called a droop-snoot, increasing camber above the leading edge and reducing it underneath. The modification hardly changed the appearance of the aircraft, but it meant that henceforth, even if a pilot tried to take off with the tail scraping the runway, he would eventually become airborne. Today this is a design requirement for all big jet transports. One can argue endlessly about whether de Havilland should have got it right the first time.

Unfortunately, serious accidents continued to happen. The next was on the first anniversary of the first scheduled service. On 2 May 1953 BOAC's 'YV departed from Calcutta with a full load of thirty-six passengers plus an infant. The experienced captain, Maurice Haddon, reported severe turbulence as he climbed – almost certainly through a giant cumulonimbus cloud – at about 10,000 ft (3 km), but carried on. Suddenly, the aircraft suffered complete structural failure, the pieces falling into a paddy field only 24 miles from Dum Dum airport. The break-up was considered to have begun with a violent download on the tailplane, and that it would have been avoided if the radar had been able to indicate severe weather.

Next, it was the turn of F–BGSC, Comet 1A '019. On 25 June 1953, flying a scheduled UAT service, it far overshot the runway when landing at Dakar. Nobody was seriously hurt, but the aircraft was a write-off.

The action then returned to Calcutta, where '04, 'YR, came to grief exactly a month later, while taxiing at Dum Dum. The Flight Safety Foundation report read:

> Because the taxi lights were too dim, the crew used the landing lights. To avoid meltdown, the lights had to be alternated, by using the switch behind the captain's seat. In a left turn, the captain took his hand off the steering wheel, to switch lights. The steering centred, and the right main gear ran off the taxiway. Power was applied to the right engines, causing the gear to be forced up through the wing, causing much damage.

The aircraft was sent to Farnborough and used for water-tank testing, as will be explained later.

On 20 October 1953 it was announced that PanAmerican World Airways had ordered an initial three Comets of a much more advanced type, designated Comet 3. This is described in the next chapter.

The next accident, the sixth, marked a turning point. On 10 January 1954, 'YP, the first production aircraft, departed from Rome, bound for London. The weather was fine, and as he neared the 35,000 ft (10,670 m) initial cruise height, Captain Gibson called a BOAC DC-4M Argonaut far below. He asked 'Did you get my…'. The question was never completed. A fisherman south of the island of Elba reported seeing the sky full of falling objects. BOAC withdrew its remaining Comets 'as a measure of prudence', and an investigation began. To the author it was obvious that to cut off the captain in mid-sentence, the catastrophe must have been instantaneous, but the extraordinary official view was that the cause was 'probably an engine fire'. After a frantic investigation, no fewer than fifty modifications were introduced, all random, and none having the slightest bearing on the actual cause.

On 23 March 1954 clearance was given to resume Comet services. On 8 April 'YY took off from Rome, heading south for Cairo. While climbing to cruising height it suffered a catastrophic accident, again too sudden for any radio transmission. The remains fell near the volcano Stromboli, into water too deep to consider salvage. This was the last straw, and all Comet 1 and 1A services were terminated.

Meanwhile, a Royal Navy salvage team had begun recovering pieces of 'YP from the seabed. They did a fantastic job, and ultimately 75 per cent of the

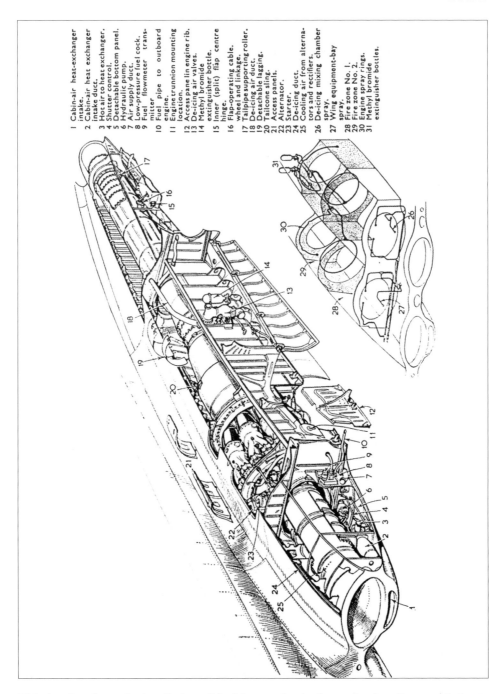

1 Cabin-air heat-exchanger intake.
2 Cabin-air heat exchanger intake duct.
3 Hot air to heat exchanger.
4 Shutter control.
5 Detachable bottom panel.
6 Hydraulic pump.
7 Air supply duct.
8 Low-pressure fuel cock.
9 Fuel flowmeter transmitter.
10 Fuel pipe to outboard engine.
11 Engine trunnion mounting location.
12 Access panel in engine rib.
13 De-icing air valves.
14 Methyl bromide extinguisher bottle.
15 Inner (split) flap centre hinge.
16 Flap-operating cable, wheel and linkage.
17 Tailpipe supporting roller.
18 De-icing air duct.
19 Detachable lagging.
20 Tailcone sling.
21 Access panels.
22 Alternator.
23 Starter.
24 De-icing duct.
25 Cooling air from alternators and rectifiers.
26 De-icing mixing chamber spray.
27 Wing equipment-bay spray.
28 Fire zone No. 1.
29 Fire zone No. 2.
30 Engine spray rings.
31 Methyl bromide extinguisher bottles.

This drawing shows the installation of the No 2 engine in the production Comet 1. A simple sketch shows the disposition of the fire-extinguishing piping in relation to the vital primary structure. *(Copyright Iliffe & Sons)* aircraft was brought back to England. The pieces were reassembled in a recon-struction at the Royal Aircraft Establishment (RAE) at Farnborough, where the Director, Sir Arnold Hall, organised an exhaustive investigation. While inspect-ing the pieces of tailplane, it was suddenly noticed that at one point the skin bore the clear imprint of a coin. Close by were neatly imprinted areas of blue bordered by gold, from the violent impact of fuselage skin. At last it was obvious that the cause had been explosive decompression of the fuselage.

Eventually, the initial failure was traced to the corner of one of the ADF antenna cut-outs in the top of the fuselage. The author was amazed that this had been a square hole, with a small corner radius, whereas engineers had known for over 100 years that any aperture in a cylindrical pressure vessel should be either circular or, better still, a transverse ellipse. To make matters worse, the square aper-ture had been reinforced by a doubler plate which, to save time, had not been Reduxed on but attached by rivets.

Bishop himself described fitting riveted doubler plates round the Comet fuse-lage apertures as 'my biggest mistake'. At one point it was even found that a crack emanating from the corner of a window had been halted by drilling a hole in the traditional way. In recent years a legend has grown up that Sir Geoffrey de Havilland himself insisted on square windows, in order to be different from the round-windowed DC-4 and Constellation, but there is no evidence to support this. More to the point, with hindsight, it can be seen that all the exhaustive fatigue testing of specimens of pressurised structure had been unrepresentative, both by the hand finishing of the parts, and the alteration of the molecular struc-ture by prior static testing.

All the remaining Comets were flown back to Hatfield, or to the RAE at Farnborough. Comet 06007, 'YU, which had made 1,230 flights, was put in a water tank at Farnborough, with the wings projecting, so that while the fuselage was subjected to repeated pressure of 1.33 times the design dP (i.e., 10.97 lb/in^2), the wings could be cycled up and down with simulated flight loads. Use of water meant that should the cabin rupture, there would be no catastrophic disintegra-tion, but merely the appearance of a crack. After 1,830 additional 'flights', the fuselage split open, the crack starting at the corner of one of the square passenger windows.

The Court of Inquiry, chaired by Lord Cohen, began sitting on 19 October 1954. My colleague Ken Owen was detailed to cover the proceedings. He returned from the first day, saying: 'It looks like it will take several more days.' In fact he had to go to Church House, Westminster, each weekday until 24 November. Soon afterwards, the seemingly endless proceedings were published in a report nearly 5 in (127 mm) thick. It reached the self-evident conclusion that 'YP had suffered explosive decompression, starting at the corner of a cut-out in the fuselage. It added that the wing had 'relatively low resistance to fatigue', that there was 'the possibility of fuel from the venting system entering the trailing-edge area near the jetpipe shrouds', and that there was 'risk of damage during refuelling the outer-wing tanks'. It also reached the much less-evident conclusion that no particular blame should be levelled at anyone, especially not at de Havilland. Apparently, it was considered that square cut-outs in a pressure vessel, and holes drilled to arrest cracks, were evidence of competent design.

Dated 11 September 1954, this photograph shows Comet 1 G-ALYU in the water tank at Farnborough, with the wings being flexed up and down. Each time the fuselage was inspected, the water was transferred to the tank in the background. *(Philip Jarrett)*

When 'YU began testing in the water tank it had made 1,221 flights. After completing a further 1,836 simulated flights the fuselage ripped open along the left side. The crack initiated at a rivet hole near the escape hatch. *(via Philip Jarrett)*

What the de Havilland company now had to do was to decide whether, in view of the worldwide publicity of the disasters, the Comet should be consigned to history, or developed into a safe vehicle with a different name, or even just a US-style numerical designation. In March 1955 the bold decision was taken to create a new, and completely safe, aircraft known as the Comet 4.

When writing this chapter, the author sought unsuccessfully for a published empty weight for the Comet 1. Eventually former de Havilland engineeer, and ex-Editor of *Flight International*, Mike Ramsden came up with the answer. At 46,300 lb it is astonishingly low, and evidence of the amazing way the Hatfield designers had pared every surplus ounce off the structure. It is fair to comment that making the whole airframe safe and fatigue-free could almost certainly have been done whilst staying under 48,000 lb, still a remarkable 45.7 per cent of the maximum take-off weight.

Ever since, the Comet disasters have generated more heat than light. Former de Havilland folk have become aggressive in rebutting any slur cast on Hatfield products. On 13 June 2002 the British television station Channel 4 screened a major probe entitled 'Comet Cover-up'. The producers brought in everyone with a possible viewpoint, including John Cunningham and the author, and produced a programme which could have been a valuable historical record. Unfortunately, it gradually became manifest that the over-riding objective of the producers was to demonstrate that de Havilland had rushed through development of the Comet in a shockingly negligent way, and this generated a justifiable storm of protest from people who had been there at the time.

This was a pity, because it tended to obscure the fact that de Havilland had built nineteen Comet 1 and 1A aircraft, of which seven had crashed in a period of 16 months, for three quite different reasons.

Chapter 4

The Comet 2 and 3

Having spent the second half of 1954 bringing almost new Comet 1s and 1As back to Hatfield, and sorting out numerous financial and legal problems, de Havilland were relieved on 12 February 1955 to find that, amazingly, the voluminous report absolved them from any blame. Just over a month later, on 20 March, the company announced the Comet 4. Shortly afterwards, in a near-rerun of the 1944 'order' for 25 D.H.106s, BOAC stated that it would order nineteen. With such an astonishing (perhaps politically motivated) expression of confidence, the design of this supposed definitive version, based on the Comet 3 and also marketed as the New Comet, went ahead at once.

Deciding what to do with surviving Comet 1s was far from easy, and there were tricky legal and financial hurdles to overcome on almost every aircraft. A more enduring problem was posed by the Comet 2. Production of these aircraft at Belfast and Chester had been halted in late-1954, and numerous supporting contracts with suppliers and customers had been either redrafted or terminated.

The immediate problem was that about twenty Comets at Chester were almost complete, or in an advanced state of construction. The main assembly hall was full of Comet 2s, initially for BOAC, and later for CPA, UAT, Air France, BCPA, JAL, LAV and Panair do Brasil. Painstaking analysis of the necessary structural modifications eventually led to the unwelcome conclusion that the cost of

F-BGNY was returned to de Havilland for a fuselage rebuild, including multi-ply skin panels with elliptical windows, becoming a Comet 1AX, G-AOJU, engaged on BOAC crew training. It later went as a Comet 1XB to Boscombe Down as XM829. *(Philip Birtles)*

reconstruction, and the increased structural weight, would make such an effort marginally not worthwhile. Thus, all the existing contracts for Comet 2 aircraft were terminated, but the decision was taken to complete a significant number for the RAF, where operating profit was not an important issue.

The Avon testbed, the Comet 2X, No.06 'YT, continued carrying out considerable test work, but was eventually retired as an instructional aircraft at the great RAF apprentice school at Halton, in Buckinghamshire. No. 23, G-ANXA, originally flown on 27 August 1953 as the first production Comet 2 for BOAC, became the first of thirteen Comet 2 aircraft for the RAF.

Meanwhile, having struck a fair deal, the Canadian Government eventually decided to take delivery, almost four years late, of the two RCAF Comet 1As, Nos. 17 and 18. In 1956 these had their fuselages almost completely rebuilt, being redesignated Comet 1XB. Redelivered in September 1957, they served reliably until October 1964 with RCAF No.412 Sqn. The externally obvious

First flown on 16 February 1952 as the Comet 2X, with early Avon engines, the sixth
Comet, G-ALYT, ended its days as an instructional airframe at RAF Halton. *(Philip Birtles)*

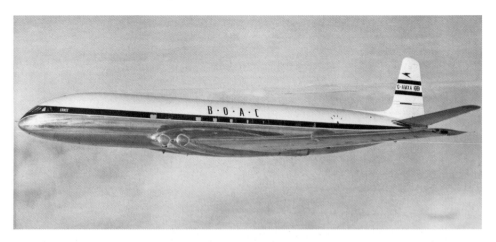

The 23rd Comet, G-AMXA, was the first production Comet 2. It is seen here on its first flight, on 27 August 1953. At that time it was 'all systems go' with Comet production. This aircraft was eventually equipped as the first RAF/Ministry Comet 2, XK655, before ending its days at the Strathallan collection, at Auchterarder. *(Philip Jarrett)*

Probably taken in May 1953, this shows the first two Comet 2 aircraft for BOAC in final assembly at Hatfield, with the first production batch of Avon Mk 504 engines in the foreground.

The 23rd Comet, G-AMXA, was the first production Comet 2. Flight testing began
on 27 August 1953. It was converted into the first Comet 2R, XK655, serving from
17 February 1958 with 51 Sqn, RAF. A handicap was the unpressurised fuselage.
(Philip Birtles)

change in these aircraft was that the passenger windows were now oval,
though, surprisingly, the major axis was not the optimum vertical but horizontal. The ADF apertures were reconstructed with generous corner radii, and
there were numerous less-evident modifications, the most important being
almost complete re-skinning of the fuselage.

Similar reconstruction of the intended BOAC Comet 2s produced a succession of aircraft which were delivered to the RAF:

06023: the first production Comet 2, originally G-AMXA, became XK655, used
  for testing and development, before being retired to RAF Shawbury, Shropshire
  in April 1968, from where it went to the Strathallan collection.
06024: originally 'XB, became XK669, initially a Comet T.2 crew trainer, and then
  a C,2. From October 1959 the Comet C.2 fleet, based at Lyneham, Wiltshire,
  were given the names of stars which at that time were important in long-range
  astro-navigation, XK669 becoming Taurus.

06025: originally 'XC, became XK659, the first Comet 2R (but the second to be delivered), with RAF designation Comet R.1; as described below, it served with 192 Sqn, which became 51 Sqn., at RAF Wyton, Cambridgeshire.

06026: originally 'XD, was flown on 20 August 1954, and later did BOAC proving trials with the original Avon 502 engines inboard but the Comet 4's Avon 524 engines outboard; it was then given Mk 117 (military 502) engines as XN453, serving at the RAE at Farnborough and Bedford on radio development.

60027: originally 'XE, became XK663, an R.1; on 13 September 1957 it was destroyed in a 192 Sqn. hangar fire at RAF Wyton.

60028: originally 'XF, became XK670, a T.2, and then a C.2, Corvus.

60029: originally 'XG, became XK671, a C.2, Aquila.

60030: originally 'XH, became XK695, a C.2, Perseus, and then an R.1 at 51 Sqn.

60031: originally 'XI, became XK696, a C.2, Orion.

60032: originally 'XJ, became XK697, a C.2, Cygnus, and then an R.1 at 51 Sqn.

60033: originally 'XK, was delivered to the Ministry of Supply, and used for Avon 524 proving trials, before becoming XV144 on blind-landing development at Bedford and Farnborough.

60034: originally 'XL, became XK698, a C.2, Pegasus.

60035: never received civil registration, and became XK699, a C.2, Sagittarius.

60036: never completed, being used for fuselage pressure testing.

60037: never received civil registration, and became XK715, a C.2, Columba.

60038–44: were never completed.

60045: was the first Comet built at Chester, being completed on 6 May 1957 as XK716, a C.2, Cepheus.

60046-49: Chester-built Comet 2 airframes which were never completed.

60100: the sole Comet 3, built at Hatfield.

The Comet C.2 fleet, which could never have been afforded on a normal RAF budget, gave exemplary service for many years with 216 Sqn. at Lyneham, Wiltshire. The first was delivered in June 1956, when the author reported to RAF Clyffe Pypard, close to Lyneham, ready to leave on a 216 proving flight to Malta early the next day. It was a struggle to get up and shave next morning, because the hospitable Clyffe Pypard mess specialised in the formidable local brew Wadworths XXX, as the author painfully remembers over half a century later!

The 17th Comet was the first of two Comet 1As for the RCAF. First flown on 21 February 1953, it is seen at Hatfield two days later in the full RCAF livery with serial number VC5301. It finally entered service as a Comet 1XB in September 1957, until retirement in October 1965. Its nose is in RCAF Rockcliffe Air Museum. *(Philip Jarrett)*

Originally intended as a BOAC Comet 2, 60033 was completed in July 1957 as one of the two Comet 2E engine development aircraft, with a completely rebuilt fuselage and Avon RA.29s in the outboard engine bays. It retained registration G-AMXK, but later became XV144. *(Philip Birtles)*

Comet 1A No 22 was delivered to Air France as F–BGNZ. After registration as G–APAS, and then as experimental G–5–23, it was taken over by the Ministry of Supply as a Comet 1XB, XM823 for special testing. It is seen on its last flight, from RAF Shawbury, on 8 April 1968.

G–AMXD, the 26th Comet off the Hatfield line, first flew as a regular Series 2 on 20 August 1954. Eventually it was modified with a fatigue-resistant fuselage, and RA.29 engines in the outboard bays. By August 1957 it was equipped as a Series 2E, for long-range radio development, serving at the RAE at Farnborough and Bedford as XN453.

Another picture of the second Comet 2E, originally G-AMXK and now totally refurnished as XV144, the principal aircraft of the Blind Landing Experimental Unit at Bedford.
It played a central role in the development of Smiths Autoland. Note the cable loop hanging under the fuselage.

Compared with the Comet 1, the principal new feature of the Comet 2 was that the engines were replaced by the Rolls-Royce Avon Mk 117, with an axial compressor, de-rated from 8,000 lb to 7,350 lb (3,334 kg). The other new feature was that the fuselage was lengthened to 96 ft (29 m), to provide room for two extra rows of seats. Like the RCAF Comet 1s, the Comet 2 aircraft for the RAF had the fuselage largely re-skinned, resulting in a significant increase in empty weight (see table of data). Another upgrade was that the fuel capacity was increased by adding a centre-section tank, holding almost 1,000 gallons. A further change was a very small increase in wing chord, and thus area.

Other changes included fitting RAF safety equipment, a fully equipped galley, and a strong damage-resistant floor for cargo, on which could be clipped up to forty-four aft-facing passenger seats. The typical 1950s RAF electronics included an Ekco nose radar, offering limited storm-warning and mapping capability, a

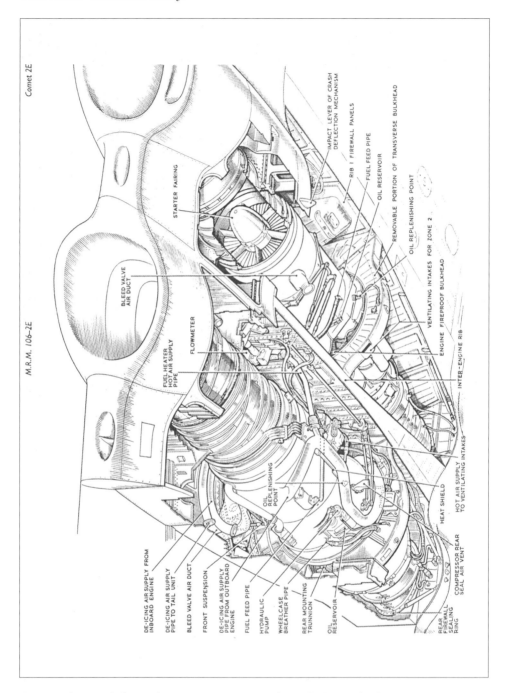

Assisting the switch from Ghost engines to Avons, the 26th Comet, built as G-AMXD, was tested with Avon RA.25 Mk 504 engines inboard and completely redesigned Avon RA.29 Mk 524 outboard. This view is looking up at engines 3 and 4.

An unusual view of an unidentified Comet C.2 of the RAF. Visible features include the engines without reversers, the fuel-jettison pipes at the trailing-edge kink, and the dinghy hatch in the wing-root trailing edge. *(Philip Jarrett)*

roof sextant (very important in the 1950s), Gee Mk 3, and an API (air-position indicator), but no DME or VOR. The SEP.2 autopilot could be set for a drift-up climb, from an initial 35,000 ft (10.7 km) to 45,000 ft (13.7 km), thereafter cruising at Mach 0.74. These reliable workhorses served until April 1967.

The Comet C.2 operations seldom made the headlines, and as far as the world at large was concerned, another version, the Comet R.1, never even existed. It never appeared in *Jane's All the World's Aircraft*, and references to it in books about the Comet have typically dismissed it as 'an electronic-calibration aircraft'. In a way this description was true, because its duties were indeed to measure signals emitted by electronic systems, but they were not British systems.

Britain has for several hundred years been a world leader in military intelligence. In the 20th Century this prowess increasingly involved electronic intelligence, and by the 1940s this branch had split into three main subdivisions: Elint (electronic intelligence), Sigint (signals) and Comint (communications). All three had played a significant part in winning the Second World War, and some of the most fascinating and exciting stories of that conflict deal with electronics. The author refers the reader to the story of how an Anson crew were refused permission to 'waste petrol' trying to prove that the *Luftwaffe* was using a radio beam to guide bombers to British cities. Risking a court-martial, the crew went out in defiance of orders, and proved it. Or how a tired Wellington Ic deliberately offered itself to a German night fighter to try to find out how an electronic aid called *Emil-Emil* worked; it ditched off Kent as a shattered wreck, with every member of the crew wounded, but with the vital knowledge needed to create countermeasures.

By the 1950s there were fewer heroics, but a rapidly growing catalogue of electronic devices. Following a succession of special Lancasters, Lincolns and Canberras, the Comet R.1 was the first platform really able to do a useful job in the modern environment of high-subsonic speeds, and altitudes up to over 40,000 ft (12 km), whilst carrying a useful array of devices and operators. The first R.1 to be delivered, on 19 April 1957, was 06027, XK663, which was unfortunately burned beyond repair inside its hangar five months later. Numerically the first, XK659, was delivered on 12 July 1957. The operating unit, 192 Sqn., was renumbered as 51 Sqn. on 21 August 1958, and remains 51 to this day, as related in Chapter 8.

Externally, the Comet R.1 looked almost exactly like a Comet C.2, at least initially. Their big drawback was that, for various reasons not only concerned with parsimonious finance, they had unmodified structures and were therefore without the benefit of pressurisation. This greatly reduced their operating height and thus their ability to 'see' long distances, and the higher fuel consumption also reduced sortie radius and duration. Flying provocative missions in someone else's airspace is not a good idea for such an unsuitable aircraft, and this obviously curtailed what 51 Sqn. could achieve. Whether the squadron's missions were integrated to replace the secret and dangerous missions, which until 1958 had been flown from RAF Sculthorpe, by USAF North American RB-45C Tornados, operated in RAF markings by joint RAF/USAF crews, has yet to be revealed.

Once it had been decided to switch to the Rolls-Royce Avon engine, it was an easier step to make use of that engine's rapid growth. In late-1952, Ian Robertson, sales manager at de Havilland Engines at Stag Lane, showed the author the first three-view drawings of not only the mighty Gyron turbojet but also an astonishingly stretched Comet with much more powerful Avon engines. At the Farnborough airshow in September 1953 this aircraft was publicly announced as the Comet 3. It promised to transform the pioneer jetliner, vastly improving its saleability, and also (in the author's opinion) making it look even better. This at last was the Comet that many airlines had waited for. Its success seemed assured when a month later, the American flag-carrier PanAm ordered three, plus a further seven on option. Others were quickly sold to BOAC and Air India.

The key to this all-new Comet was the engine. Previous 100-series Avons had a 12-stage compressor which tapered to feed the eight tubular combustion chambers, typical mass flow being 119 lb (54 kg) per second. The Comet 3's Avon 200-series had a redesigned 15-stage compressor, with better aerodynamics, which did not taper but led to a can-annular combustion chamber. The result was an engine with a decreased diameter, despite an increase in airflow to an initial 150 lb (68 kg) per second, a figure soon improved upon. Thus, whereas Comet 2 Avons were typically rated at 7,350 lb, or less, the Comet 3 began with the Avon Mk 521 at the RA.26 rating of 10,000 lb (4,536 kg). This was a mere 10 in (254 mm) longer than the engine of the Comet 2, so it still fitted between the Comet's wing spars, and its weight of 2,790 lb (1,265 kg) was a modest increase of 370 lb. The first 200-series engine went on test at Derby on 17 November 1951, and it was soon in production, initially for the Valiant bomber.

Visibly, the chief change in the Comet 3 installation was that the air inlets had become large near-rectangles, in order to handle the much greater airflow. Also obvious was the extension of the jetpipes to well behind the wing, with increased outward curvature. The Comet 3 did not make more noise on take-off than a Mk 1, but environmental issues were just beginning to be important. For several years, a Rolls-Royce team at Hucknall, near Nottingham, led by F.B. Greatrex, had experimented with methods of reducing noise on take-off. Work centred on increasing the periphery of the jet, in order to achieve more rapid mixing with the surrounding air. The eventual answer was an expanding nozzle fitted with six peripheral chutes, which induced surrounding air to mix quickly with the jet. By modern standards, the noise on take-off was still unacceptable.

A different problem was to try to make a turbojet give 'reverse thrust' to help to arrest an aircraft after landing, especially on an icy runway. Cutting a long story short, the eventual answer at Rolls-Royce was to install inside the jetpipe upper and lower curved shutters, each pivoted across a diameter. Normally these shutters rested flush inside the jetpipe. On landing, the pilot pulled back the throttle levers, armed the reversers by pulling up a selector lever on the front of each throttle, and then moved the throttle levers firmly down (the reverse of that on take-off). This restored high power, while the curved doors closed to shut off

Taken on 9 September 1954, this photograph shows the Comet 3 nearest the camera. In the rear is the fourth production Comet 2, G-AMXD, which had first flown on 20 August. Ultimately 'XD was to go to the Ministry of Supply as XN453, seen again in the next photograph. *(Philp Jarrett)*

the jetpipes, forcing the jet to escape through upper and lower apertures, fitted with curved cascade vanes. These directed the jets diagonally forward, above and below the wing, giving reverse thrust.

Trials with reverse thrust began in 1954, using an Avon in a test cell. Then 'YT, the Comet 2X, was fitted with an improved reverser behind the No.1 (left outer) Avon RA.9 engine. Astonishingly, this reverser was fixed in the open (reverse) position, so each take-off had to be made with this engine at idle power. After a three-engined approach, on touchdown No.1 was opened to full power. Despite the sheer crudity of the arrangement, it demonstrated that the Comet could be kept straight, without tyre scrubbing or hot-gas reingestion. Operable reversers were eventually fitted to the Comet 4 family, but on the outboard engines only, to avoid buffeting the fuselage.

Here XN453 is seen in the background, after being partly rebuilt as the first of two Comet 2Es, equipped for research into navaids, with side and ventral sensor blisters. In the foreground is the unique seventh Comet 4, delivered to BOAC as G-APDF on the last day of 1958. It later was leased to Air Ceylon before going to the Ministry of Aviation as XN814, based at RAE Bedford. When this picture was taken it was testing the special receivers for the Nimrod R.1. Later, with the pannier removed, and painted in Raspberry ripple, it tested the tail of the Nimrod MRA.4 before being scrapped on 12 August 1997. *(Philip Jarrett)*

Recognising that the much greater engine thrust now available could match an aircraft of considerably increased weight, the obvious next step was to increase fuel capacity. Internal fuel was slightly increased, the problem being lack of available volume, and the reluctant decision was taken to add fuel externally. Viewed by some airlines as a visibly retrograde step, the Comet 3 appeared with what was called a 'pinion tank' projecting prominently ahead of each outer wing. The name came from the similarly disposed claws on birds of prey. This odd answer, which was tested on the second Comet 1, 'ZK, enabled capacity to be increased to 8,308 gallons, a total which was later increased to 8,750 gallons (10,508 US gallons, 39,778 litres).

In 1952 de Havilland began building the prototype Comet 3, serial 06100, leaving a big serial-number gap for hoped-for Comet 2s, as listed previously. Construction also proceeded on a static-test airframe, and assisted by Chester and Belfast, on an initial batch of production Series 3 aircraft, which began selling strongly. The prototype was registered G-ANLO, and began flight testing on 19 July 1954, at a time when de Havilland was completely preoccupied with Comet 1 accidents. Though the Comet 3 was not affected by the grounding of the Comet 1 fleet, the decision was quickly taken to abandon it, and to put every effort into developing it into a demonstrably safe Comet 4.

Chapter 5

The Comet 4 Family

The decision of March 1955 to go ahead with a supposedly completely safe Comet 4 put the Hatfield management in a difficult position. Whereas in 1949 the first Comet had been the only jet transport in the world, by 1955 the French were testing the attractive Caravelle, while Boeing and Douglas had announced that they were building jet airliners which would be faster, more capacious and longer-ranged than any Comet, and that these would enter service in 1958 and 1959. Indeed, in 1956, Aeroflot, the civil air organisation of the Soviet Union, put into service a totally unexpected jet transport, the Tu-104, derived from the Tu-16 bomber, though this had only a small impact on the world airline scene. To make a success of the now much-delayed programme, de Havilland had to move very quickly. In the event, making the seemingly trivial changes needed to turn the Comet 3 into the Comet 4 took as long as Boeing and Douglas needed to create their all-new 'Big Jets' from scratch.

In parallel with work on these so-called New Comets, the unique Comet 3 was brought almost up to Comet 4 standard, and, having lost three years, resumed test flying on 25 February 1957. The engines were now Avon RA.29 Mk.523s, rated at 10,500 lb (4,763 kg), and G-ANLO was sufficiently like a Comet 4 to complete much of the ARB (Air Registration Board) certification. When the first Series 4, 06401 G-APDA, flew on 27 April 1958, most of the work had already been signed off. This aircraft was followed by 06402, which was a structural-test airframe.

Structurally, the Comet 4 was a Comet 3 incorporating the changes already in production for the Comet 2, with a reskinned fuselage with generous radii in every cut-out. The propulsion system differed only in that the engine was the Avon Mk 524, at the RA.29 rating of 10,500 lb (4,763 kg), which had been tested on the Comet 2X. This increase in thrust was achieved by adding a zero-stage, an extra stage of blading on the front of the compressor, which increased mass flow as well as pressure ratio. All four engines were fitted with Greatrex noise-reducing nozzles, and Nos. 1 and 4 had reversers.

With a fuel capacity, including the pinion tanks, finally increased to 8,908 gal (40,496 lit, 10,698 US gal), the Comet 4 achieved a no-reserves, still-air range of 4,030 miles (6,485 km), and thus was almost, but not quite, suit-

The Comet 3B is seen here at RAE Bedford, serving at the BLEU with a long nose probe feeding the instrumentation. Previously registered G-ANLO, the Ministry serial number was XP915.

After being converted from a Comet 3 into a 3B, G-ANLO is seen here in 1959 in
BEA livery.

able for the North Atlantic. The extra fuel increased MTO weight to 162,000
lb (73,493 kg). The British national airline BOAC, having announced that it
would use the turboprop Britannia for all its long-haul routes, and had no
interest in the Vickers 1000 – an aircraft already being built for the RAF, in
the class of the 707 and DC-8 – caused uproar by ordering fifteen Boeing
707s, powered by the same engines as the Vickers 1000. The second Comet 4,
G-APDB, No.06403, was delivered to BOAC on 30 September 1958. It was
rushed into flying the first scheduled transatlantic jet service on 4 October.
Despite being designed for shorter routes, BOAC was determined to use
the Comet 4 to beat PanAm with its Boeing 707-121. The US airline began
transatlantic operations on 26 October, and since then the author has had a
plastic bag proclaiming 'Jet Clipper passenger'. It was a childish ploy to put
the Comet 4 on the North Atlantic, and it was replaced as soon as BOAC's
707–436 fleet were delivered.

Almost all the Comet 4s had quite long careers with a succession of operators, though, as most major flag carriers had bought the 707 or DC-8, most

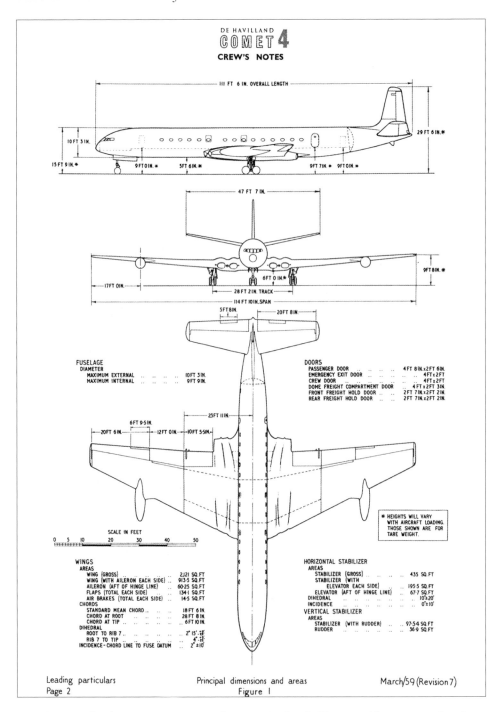

DE HAVILLAND
COMET 4
CREW'S NOTES

Leading particulars
Page 2

Principal dimensions and areas
Figure 1

March/59 (Revision 7)

Crew's Notes for the Comet 4 was actually a massive book. Fig. 1 provides a comprehensive review of external dimensions.

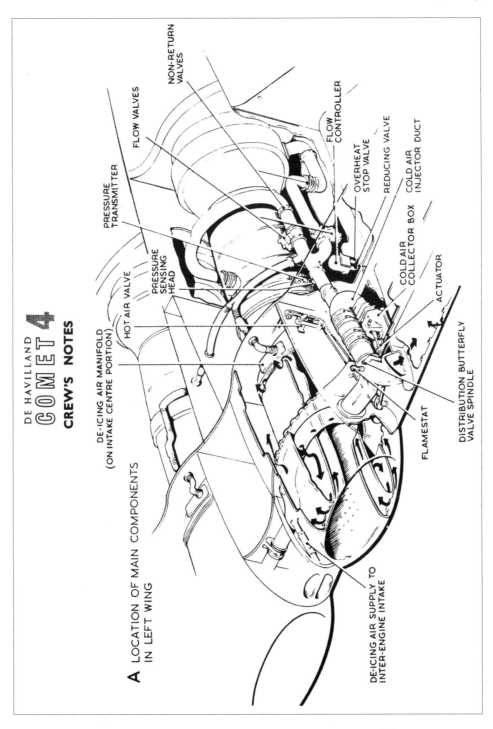

DE HAVILLAND
COMET 4
CREW'S NOTES

A LOCATION OF MAIN COMPONENTS IN LEFT WING

DE-ICING AIR MANIFOLD (ON INTAKE CENTRE PORTION)

PRESSURE TRANSMITTER

FLOW VALVES

NON-RETURN VALVES

FLOW CONTROLLER

OVERHEAT STOP VALVE

REDUCING VALVE

COLD AIR INJECTOR DUCT

PRESSURE SENSING HEAD

HOT AIR VALVE

COLD AIR COLLECTOR BOX

ACTUATOR

FLAMESTAT

DISTRIBUTION BUTTERFLY VALVE SPINDLE

DE-ICING AIR SUPPLY TO INTER-ENGINE INTAKE

This diagram shows secondary flows around the Comet 4 No 1 engine (left outer) of them were in the third world. As noted later, an upstart British operator, Dan-Air, built up an astonishing Comet fleet, including several Comet 4s. One of the last Comet 4s to remain airworthy was 06419, G-APDS, which, after service with BOAC, Air Ceylon and Kuwait Airways, was sold in January 1969 to the Ministry of Defence. It became XW626, still just designated as a Comet 4, and began work as a trials aircraft at the A&AEE (Aeroplane & Armament Experimental Establishment), at Boscombe Down. In late-1971 this aircraft went to the Chester factory, for a major conversion to test the nose-mounted radar proposed for an AEW Nimrod. The rest of the story is related in Chapter 9.

Back in the mid-1950s there were a few bright spots, one being the announcement by Capital Airlines in July 1956 that it would buy four Comet 4s and ten Comet 4As. Capital, based in Washington DC, had been delighted with the British turboprop Viscount – reminding its staff 'pronounced Vi-count' – and said that the Comet would for the second time enable it to beat its rivals, this time by being first with jets. Delighted, de Havilland quickly went ahead with the 4A, with a structure modified to carry more passengers over shorter ranges, at increased indicated airspeeds. Visible changes included a third stretch to the fuselage, to 114 ft 10 in (35 m), increasing seating to ninety-two, and removal of the outer wing panels to reduce span to 107 ft 9½ in (32.86 m). Unseen was local strengthening of the structure, especially the tail. The pinion tanks were retained, and gross weight remained at the original Comet 4 level of 152,500 lb. Unfortunately, Capital soon vanished into mighty United, which was already buying DC-8s, and the Capital order was cancelled.

However, by this time British European Airways (BEA) was talking about buying a similar aircraft, and in April 1958 the airline signed for six, later increasing this number to fourteen. Designated as the Comet 4B, this version was basically a Comet 4A, but with the fuselage stretched for the fourth time, to 118 ft (35.97 m), and powered by Avon 525B engines, again rated at 10,500 lb. Professing to be disgusted, Georges Hereil, President of France's Sud-Aviation, commented:

> The BEA Comet will cost much more than the Caravelle, though it will carry the same number of passengers for the same distance at the same speed, using the same engine, but with four engines instead of two!

G-APMA, the first Comet 4B for BEA, is seen taking off from Hatfield on 14 July 1959. It had first flown on 27 June. *(Phil Jarrett)*

In fact, the Comet 4B actually cruised fractionally faster than a Caravelle, because the outer wings were redesigned and the pinion tanks removed. It also had a greater payload, because the fuselage was further stretched, to be 78 in (1.98 m) longer than the Comet 4, later enabling seating to reach 119. Despite losing the pinion tanks, the range with maximum payload was still 3,350 miles (5,390 km), ample for BEA's European routes.

On the other hand, the Comet 4 was an excellent aircraft for the Far East and Africa, and de Havilland completed wringing out more from the same basic design with the Comet 4C. This quite logically mated the high-capacity fuselage of the 4B with the wing of the 4, and had it appeared several years earlier might have sustained major production. In fact only thirty were

XR396, c/n 06468, the second of five Comet C.4s built for the RAF. Based at Lyneham, they never carried names, but gave trouble-free service from 1962 to 1975, when they were sold to Dan-Air and refurnished as civil Comet 4Cs. This one became G-BDIU. *(Phil Jarrett)*

constructed, twenty-three of them at Chester, including one for King Ibn Saud of Saudi Arabia, five for the RAF, and one for electronic testing. Two were left unsold, and these feature in Chapter 9.

New 4C Comets were sold to Mexicana, Egyptair (at the time of the order called Misrair, and then United Arab Airways), Middle East, Sudan, Aerolineas and Kuwait. In 1966 the small British independent carrier Dan-Air bought two Comet 4s from BOAC. Over the next seven years it acquired a total of no fewer than thirty-eight Comet 4, 4B and 4C aircraft, resulting in this little inclusive-tour and charter company having the biggest ever Comet fleet. Like other Comet operators, Dan-Air fairly quickly replaced its Comets with aircraft of later design, its last Comet service being an enthusiast charter from Gatwick to Dusseldorf on 9 November 1980.

The five RAF aircraft, designated Comet C.4, with serials XR 395–399, were basically standard 4Cs, with RAF avionics and 94 aft-facing seats. The first went on test on 15 November 1961, and the first delivery, to 216 Sqn. at Lyneham, was on 9 February 1962. All five were later sold to Dan-Air.

There are many websites offering different aspects of the D.H.106 Comet. One lists twenty-one Comets of which at least a number still survive; of these, nine are essentially complete aircraft. Another site, in Russian, credits the Comet's genesis to a Lord Barbizon.

Chapter 6

The Nimrod MR.1

Today it is difficult to believe that, on 4 April 1957, the British Minister of Defence, Duncan Sandys, made the astonishing announcement that the Royal Air Force would be 'unlikely to require' any new fighters or bombers – at any time in the future – and that 'work on such projects will therefore stop.' In his opinion, future wars would be fought entirely by missiles. At the time, the author was the Chairman of the Circle of Aviation Writers, and the Circle's next off-the-record lunch guest was the Chief of the Air Staff. He commented: 'I wonder if I will still be allowed to wear my wings.' Mr Sandys was soon elevated to become Lord Duncan Sandys.

When the Air Staff had recovered from the shock, they realised that almost the only type of aircraft that they were still permitted to think about was one to replace the Lockheed Neptune and eventually, the Avro Shackleton, in the maritime reconnaissance (MR) role. However, as a member of the North Atlantic Treaty Organisation (NATO), the United Kingdom was ostensibly bound to participate in NATO discussions, and to agree common procurement decisions with its allies.

Just 12 days later, on 16 April, a multinational panel of experts met to consider how best to replace the Neptune as the principal MR aircraft of six NATO air forces, including the UK. This laudable objective had already been compromised by two nations which did not wait for an agreement. The US

Navy selected the Lockheed P3V, later redesignated as the P-3, Orion, powered by four turboprops. Canada adopted the Canadair CL-28 Argus, powered by four Turbo-Compound piston engines. Undaunted, the European NATO nations wrote their own Operational Requirement (OR), which was released to manufacturers on 21 March 1958. It did not specify the type of propulsion, but expected the final choice to be a turboprop. Britain's official view was that, as a member of NATO, it would accept whatever aircraft was chosen. Privately, it decided that there was plenty of time in which to take a decision, and moreover, that it would not be bound by any NATO decision, but would pursue a national solution.

On 21 October 1958 the winner of the OR was announced as the Breguet (later Dassault-Breguet) Br.1150 Atlantic, powered by two Rolls-Royce Tyne turboprops. By this time, it was clear that the UK was no longer 'on board'. Back in 1957 A.V. Roe (Avro), the company which had produced the Shackleton, had decided that the best national answer to the MR Requirement was the Avro 745, an aircraft like an upgraded 'Shack', powered by four Rolls-Royce Dart turboprops. This did not progress beyond a drawing and for the next two years, design studies for a British MR aircraft went ahead at several companies, most eagerly at A.V.Roe and de Havilland Aircraft.

It was a time of Government-enforced turmoil. A.V.Roe was about to become part of the newly created Hawker Siddeley Avro Whitworth Division, with its main production factory at Chadderton, Lancashire, between Manchester and Oldham, and the design office and airfield at Woodford, Cheshire. At Woodford, work was transferred from the Avro 745 to the Avro 775, which closely resembled a Br.1150 Atlantic, but with a Rolls-Royce RB.168 Spey turbofan added in the tail to boost maximum speed. This study was followed by a large swept-wing jet, the Avro 776, powered by three RB.178 turbofans grouped at the tail. Meanwhile, the former de Havilland team at Hatfield based their studies on the airframe of the original D.H.121 Trident passenger aircraft, powered by three Rolls-Royce RB.141 Medway turbofans.

Had either of these projects gone quickly ahead, in the author's opinion there is a fair chance that developed versions would have sold to many countries, pre-empting today's Boeing P-8A Poseidon by over 40 years. Unfortunately, the Air Staff and Ministry experts ran true to form, and did little but talk for six further years, after which time they had frittered away any prospect of creating an optimised all-new aircraft. In 1963, without any prior discussion with industry, the Air Staff issued a challenging Air Staff Target, AST.357. This called for an advanced jet aircraft, but the wasted time meant that it had to be met by either an existing type of aircraft, or something based on an existing type.

By this time the stark idiocy of the Trident's customer, British European Airways, in demanding that this aircraft should be redesigned to be much smaller, and shorter-ranged, with lower-powered RB.163 Spey engines, had not only left the world market for such aircraft to the Boeing 727, but had also eliminated the Trident as a basis for AST.357. The design teams at Woodford and Hatfield did briefly study how the emasculated Trident could be fitted with a deep stores pannier under the fuselage, in order to serve as the basis for what had become the HS.800. It was an obvious non-starter; the fuselage was too small, and despite adding Comet-style pinion tanks, this project also had totally inadequate range, like the Trident 1. A three-view appears on page 80.

Desperate to rescue something from the shambles, in June 1964 the Air Staff issued Air Staff Requirement (ASR) 381, calling for a less-advanced aircraft (so long as it could be justified as being better than the Atlantic). Money was to be saved by reusing many items of equipment taken from the Shackletons. This typical Treasury-imposed decision guaranteed that whatever aircraft was chosen, it would soon have to be completely refitted. In any case, by this time the only possible answer appeared to be to base the ASR.381 aircraft on the Comet 4C.

At first, this appeared to be a retrograde step, in view of the age of the basic design. However, as soon as the resulting studies threw up answers, it was discovered that the geriatric Comet airframe was not a bad starting point at all. By July 1964 the Woodford team, assisted by Hatfield, had completed a detailed proposal for an MR Comet, designated as the HS.801, with the Avon turbojets replaced by Rolls-Royce Spey turbofans, and with a large unpressurised addition to the fuselage, under the main floor, mainly to house a capacious weapons bay.

By this time, the HS.801 was the clear favourite, but the rival British Aircraft Corporation had also decided to compete. In autumn 1964 a BAC team, that had previously been Vickers-Armstrongs (Aircraft), provided a turboprop Vanguard and a turbofan-engined VC10 to fly simulated missions from RAF St Mawgan, near Newquay in Cornwall, in direct competition with a

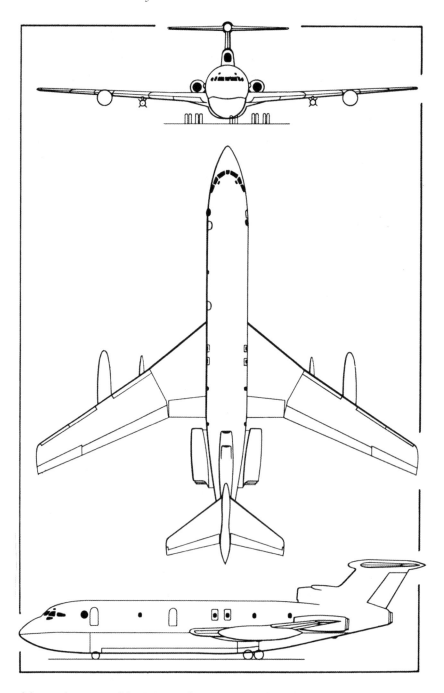

One of the predecessors of the HS.801, the HS.800 was based on the Trident 1, and from the outset was inadequate. Bizarrely, it bore a close comparison with the Boeing P-8A Poseidon of nearly half a century later.

Trident and a Comet 4C. The parameters studied included flight performance (especially range and endurance), low-level handling and ride comfort, interior noise and vibration, and accommodation for the exceptional amount of mission equipment.

A decision in principle to select the HS.801 was reached in December 1964, and a go-ahead was announced in February 1965. This was hardly a breakneck pace, furthermore, the contract was not actually signed until January 1966. Priced at £96 million, it covered the purchase of 38 HS.801 aircraft, to be designated Nimrod MR.1, after the biblical 'mighty hunter'. Slightly later, a contract was signed for three more aircraft, to be completed as Elint (electronic intelligence) platforms, designated as the Nimrod R.1, as related in Chapter 8. In order 'to bring Nimrod squadrons up to strength' an additional eight MR.1 aircraft were ordered in January 1972. Thus, the programme originally comprised:

> XV226–263 (initial batch), XZ280–287 (built to a slightly later standard), MR.1,
>   total 46; of these, 11 aircraft, XV259, XV261–263, XZ280–283, XZ285–287, were
>   later allocated for conversion to the Nimrod AEW.3 (see Chapter 9).
> XW664–666, Nimrod R.1, total 3 (see Chapter 8).

These forty-nine aircraft were assembled at Woodford. They were conveniently preceded by the last two Comet 4Cs, 06476–7, which were stored at Chester, almost complete, but unsold. By this time the sprawling Hawker Siddeley Aviation companies had sorted themselves out and put everyone in his place. Though the Comet had been a de Havilland aircraft, with the design team at Hatfield, the strong men at the Avro Whitworth Division made it very clear that they were now taking the decisions. One of their first acts was to have Comet production tooling moved from Chester and Hatfield to Woodford. Henceforth 'Mr Nimrod' was Gilbert Whitehead, the Woodford Executive Director and Chief Engineer.

By this time the general advance of technology had reduced the MR style of aircraft to become a mere vehicle. In this case, most of the development task of the basic aircraft had been done for the Comet. For the Nimrod, the difficulty, and the principal development task, lay in the numerous sensors and systems. Whitehead proclaimed: 'The computer calculates and displays, and the man decides what action to take,' and even on today's Nimrod MRA.4 this is still broadly true. However, in such a fast-moving technology, major strategic decisions can soon look mistaken, though at the time there may have been no real alternative.

By far the most important of these decisions, driven entirely by lack of money, was to give the Nimrod a broadly traditional cockpit, based on that of the Comet 4, with dial instruments and match a primitive digital computer with analogue avionics, many of the items even being removed from the Shackletons. This primitive equipment placed heavy demands on the aircrew, and also ensured that long before the Nimrod airframes had run out of hours, they would have to be largely gutted and equipped with a new radar and partly digital avionics. What nobody then expected was that, another 30 years further on, a small number of the same airframes would undergo a total reconstruction.

Even before the signing of the main contract, it had been decided that the last two Comets would play a major role in creating the Nimrod. The first, 06476, would become XV147, charged with the immense task of integrating the mission avionics and related equipment. The engines and general aircraft systems were left unchanged, though the additional avionics required four times as much electrical power as in a normal Comet 4C. The rather clumsy answer was to mount four 60-kVA alternators in external air-cooled pods, under the engine bays, shaft-driven via bevel gears by the Avon engines.

In contrast, the second testbed, XV148, had none of the new mission systems but differed in that the fuselage was fitted with an early design of Nimrod weapons-bay and pannier, and the powerplant bays were modified to house the new engines, the Rolls-Royce Spey Mk 250 turbofan. Though XV148 looked totally unlike a Comet, it was actually relatively simple, and so it was the first to fly. John Cunningham, who had masterminded Comet flight-testing from the beginning, flew up to Chester on The Gold Block Airline – the inter-factory shuttle with Doves, and later 125s, which later linked Airbus plants – and accompanied by the Avro Whitworth Director of Flight Test, Jimmy Harrison, began Nimrod flight-testing on 23 May 1967.

Early flight testing showed a need to increase the size of the dorsal fin, to balance the deeper forward fuselage. Still lacking many equipment items, XV147 followed on 31 July 1967. Each maiden flight ended at Woodford, again marking the change of 'centre of gravity' away from de Havilland. The first Nimrod MR.1, XV226, flew at Woodford on 28 June 1968, all subsequent testing being managed by Harrison.

The cockpit of a Nimrod MR.1, seen here, would be immediately familiar to the pilot of a wartime Lancaster, but almost completely alien to the pilot of a Nimrod MRA.4. Engine 'clocks' are grouped in the centre. *(Phil Jarrett)*

One of the first photographs of a Nimrod in flight, this perfect plan view of XV226 was taken on a slow flypast with take-off flap. *(Phil Jarrett)*

Compared with the Avon Mk 525, the Spey Mk 250 had a similar diameter but was shorter, at 117 in (2,972 mm), compared with 134 in (3,404 mm). Despite the heavy alternator, it was also significantly lighter, at 2,740 lb (1,243 kg), compared with 3,428 lb (1,555 kg). Take-off rating was raised from the Avon's 10,150 lb (45,13 kN) to an initial 12,140 lb (54 kN), with a guaranteed minimum of 11,995 lb (53,36 kN). Subsequently, the T-O rating was cleared at 12,500 lb (55,6 kN). Even more important was that specific fuel consumption at the T-O rating was reduced from the Avon's 0.87 to only 0.58, making an enormous difference to mission radius of action. This, coupled with the discovery that oceanic searches could be made with one, or even two engines shut down, transformed the available mission endurance.

The first Nimrod MR.1, on a test from Woodford in September 1968, three months after beginning flight testing. Note the beautifully uncluttered exterior.

Whereas in 1957 Rolls-Royce could proclaim that the Avon RA.29 was the first jet engine with a TBO (time between overhauls) of 1,000 hours, today most mature gas-turbine engines are overhauled 'on condition', and in airline service are often left on the airframe for 30,000 hours or more. Another advantage of modern turbofans is that, whereas in a turbojet such as the Avon, the white-hot gas is in contact with the outer casing, in a turbofan it is surrounded by a relatively cool airflow. Another advantage of the Spey was that different versions quickly gained important civil and military applications, enabling the engine to mature rapidly.

The Spey 250 had to be marinised, to avoid gradual corrosion from salt-water atmosphere. This involved extensive coating with anti-corrosive material, which for many items was pure aluminium, and total exclusion of magnesium alloys. As noise was not an issue, the jet nozzles were plain tubes, sized for optimum propulsive efficiency. The inboard pipes, from engines 2 and 3, curved outwards, while the jetpipes from engines 1 and 4 were fitted with reversers, and pointed

XV247 was the 22nd MR.1 of the original batch. It is seen here just before delivery.
(Phil Jarrett)

directly aft. Starting was by an air-turbine motor, fed from a Lucas (originally Rover) turboshaft APU (auxiliary power unit) in the fuselage tailcone.

Structurally, the airframe required considerable modification, compared with that of the Comet. The fuselage was reduced in length by cutting out a 6 ft (1.8 m) bay ahead of the wing, before reinforcing the cabin floor to withstand pressurisation loads, and adding the large unpressurised under-floor weapon-bay structure, as well as the nose radome and numerous new doors and hatches. The flight-deck window area was increased, and the passenger windows were replaced by a small number of oval windows, three of them bulged outwards to facilitate visual searches. The tail end was modified to terminate in a long MAD boom, described later. The tail was generally strengthened, and the fin modified with a dorsal extension, and a large ESM (electronic support measures) antenna fairing on top. The engine inlets were enlarged yet again, to match the increased propulsive airflow. The engine bays were little changed geometrically, but were opened up vertically to make room for the bigger engine ducts, and strengthened to withstand the greater bending moments and tensile stresses resulting from the increased maximum weight. At 192,000 lb (87,091 kg), this was almost double that of a Comet 1, and it also required strengthening of the main landing gears, and an increase in tyre pressure to 185 lb/sq in (13 kg/cm²).

Though based on those of the Comet 4C, the accessory systems showed many changes. Fuel capacity was increased yet again, by adding so-called keel tanks in the fuselage, the new total being 10,730 gallons (48 779 litres, 12,886 US gallons, c85,000 lb, 38,556 kg). For ferrying, six tanks could be carried in the weapons bay, to bring maximum fuel to 100,940 lb (45,786 kg), almost the weight of a fully loaded Comet 1.

The hydraulic systems were extended to operate additional systems, such as the doors to the weapons bay and camera apertures. As already noted, electric generating capacity was quadrupled, to 240 kVA, the four oil-cooled brush-less alternators being mounted directly on the engines via an English Electric CSD (constant-speed drive). Two Ni-Cd batteries provided increased storage capacity. The maximum cabin differential pressure was increased to 8¾ lb/sq in (0.61 kg/cm²), and the fresh-air ducting was rearranged. Bleed-air heating was extended to serve the complete weapons bay, and individual outlets were provided for crew stations.

Whereas the 'Shack' had had to provide for a supernumerary crew, with rest bunks, the Nimrod's much higher speed meant that few missions lasted as long as 12 hours, making such provision usually unnecessary. The normal crew thus numbered twelve. On the flight deck were the pilot (by no means always the captain of the aircraft), co-pilot and flight engineer. Behind was a toilet, aft of which was the main tactical compartment. This provided stations for the routine and tactical navigators, radio operator, radar operator, two SSOs (sonic-systems operators), ESM/MAD (explained later) operator, and two observer/stores loaders. At the rear was a galley, and a four-seat dining area, behind which was a spacious compartment housing sonobuoys, markers, launchers and other mission equipment. If necessary, some of the interior installations could be quickly removed, to make room for forty-five fully armed troops, or fifty-five with reduced kit.

The avionics bore little resemblance to those of the Comet. The autopilot was the Smiths SEP.6, integrated with the tac./nav. system. Primary navaids were a Decca 67M doppler, integrated with a Marconi-Elliott E3 inertial platform, with reversionary true heading being provided by a duplicate Sperry GM7 gyro-compass system. These all provided inputs to a Ferranti

RDD (routine dynamic display), which incorporated an electro-mechanical computer. Among other things, the RDD projected the aircraft's position and track on to a table, on which the routine navigator could spread any selected RAF chart. At the time, in the late 1960s, the whole system – more complex in fact than can be described here – was welcomed as state-of-the-art. Looking back from the new century, it seems archaic!

Seated beside the routine nav., the tac. nav. was the central figure in most war-like operations. The Marconi-Elliott nav./attack system centred around the 920B digital computer, and today it is hard to believe that its 8k memory was considered wonderful. A new capability was that either pilot could couple the computer to the flight-control system, or to the autopilot, enabling the tac. nav., to in effect, fly the aircraft, at least in the horizontal plane. Key elements of the system were imported, including the Emerson ASQ-10A MAD (magnetic-anomaly detector) in the tail boom. This was used for finding and tracking submarines, by measuring unnatural local distortions in the Earth's magnetic field. A Canadian Aviation Electronics nine-term compensator eliminated any spurious MAD signals generated by the aircraft itself.

Other equipment included the Thomson-CSF ESM (electronic support measures) package on top of the fin, a Strong Electric 70-million candlepower searchlight (steered by the co-pilot) in the nose of the right-hand pinion tank, and electronic-flash equipment by Chicago Aero Industries. The last-named worked in conjunction with the F126 and two F135 day/night cameras in the bottom of the rear fuselage, supplied by a British firm, Aeronautical & General Instruments. As originally built, most Nimrods had an Autolycus 'sniffer' for diesel exhaust, mounted in the roof of the flight deck. These items, removed from Shackletons, were later discarded, reflecting the replacement of older oceanic submarines by later types, with nuclear propulsion.

A Sonics 1C display showed returns from the mainly American sonobuoys (listed in the next chapter), while a British firm, Computing Devices, supplied the control panels for sonobuoy selection and release, and weapons-bay stores loading. Not least, the radar was the prehistoric ASV-21D, originally supplied by EMI for the Shackleton, but this was regarded as very much an interim solution, the radome being able to accommodate a more modern set, with a larger scanner.

What might be termed domestic avionics included duplicate Plessey PTR.175 u.h.f./v.h.f. radios, Marconi-Elliott AD.470 h.f. (providing global coverage),

AD.360 ADF and AD.260 VOR/ILS, Hoffman ARN-72 Tacan, Decca ADL-21 C/A Loran, Honeywell APN-171(V) radar altimeters (vital in most missions) and an automatic yaw damper and Mach trim. Not part of the original specification, Nimrod crews soon took to bringing an Agiflite 70-mm roll-film camera on board. Hand-held in one of the blisters, this was found invaluable for recording the name and intimate details of targets of interest and it was eventually made an official sensor.

No less than 48 ft 6 in (14.78 m) long, the weapons bay was closed by front and rear pairs of doors and could be heated. It was designed to accommodate almost every conventional store used by the RAF, arranged in six rows, to a total weight of 13,500 lb (6,124 kg). Possible loads included nine torpedoes, or 1,000 lb (454 kg) bombs, or various mines or depth charges. The wing rib at the junction of the flap and aileron provided attachments for a pylon matched to air-to-surface missiles, such as AS.12 or Martel, as well as rocket launchers or cannon pods, but the necessary launchers were never attached until the aircraft had become Nimrod MR.2s.

The aft 30 ft (9.14 m) of the pressure cabin was equipped with two rotary launchers, mounted vertically or inclined in the floor. With the interior depressurised, each launcher could eject up to six Size-A active or passive sonobuoys, or marine markers. When the aircraft was pressurised, stores could be ejected from a single tube.

Nimrod MR.1 deliveries began on 2 October 1969, initially to the MOCU (Maritime Operational Conversion Unit), which was soon renamed No.236 OCU, at St Mawgan, Cornwall. They continued to 42 Sqn. at the same location, Nos.120, 201 and 206 at Kinloss, Morayshire, Scotland, and No.203 at Luqa, Malta. A permanent detachment was rotated from the above squadrons to Tengah, Singapore. In 1979 the British withdrawal from Malta, which had been planned many years earlier, rendered the newly delivered second batch of eight Nimrods instantly redundant. They returned to the UK, where seven were later converted into Nimrod AEW.3s (see Chapter 9).

From the start it was clear that the new aircraft was far preferable to the 'Shack', not the least of its attributes being that it could make long oceanic patrols with two engines actually shut down, and at light weights could climb on one engine to about 5,000 ft (1,524 m). However, the Nimrod MR.1 was typically British in that, developed on the proverbial shoestring, it lacked numerous items which it

Taken in spring 1968, this view of the assembly line at Woodford shows it loaded with MR.1 aircraft to the full production rate. Today this building, which assembled Lancasters, Shackletons and Vulcans, has probably neared the end of plane-making. (*Phil Jarrett*).

was hoped eventually to incorporate. Subsequent upgrades and conversions are discussed in the remaining chapters.

To say that the Nimrod was welcomed is a massive understatement, but that is partly because the Shackleton was so cramped and deafening – as the author experienced several times. In contrast, he flew just once in a Nimrod MR.1, in 1976. At that time, one of his assignments was as European Editor for the monthly magazine *Aircraft*, published in Melbourne. The RAAF was considering whether to replace the Neptune with the Nimrod or the Lockheed Orion, so the author was asked to present himself at 236 OCU. Here he was invited to join a nine-hour mission. It was eventful; at one point experiencing an exciting conflagration (someone had stuffed the oven with hot-cross buns and forgotten about them). The mission ended with various pilot training circuits, and, as so many years have gone by, it may now be permissible to report that Chief Instructor Sqn. Ldr. Dick Bean, permitted the author to make a touch-and-go, overshoot with engines 3 and 4 at flight idle, and then make the final landing. His obvious enthusiasm for the Nimrod in the *Aircraft* article did not persuade the Australians to select it.

In January 1970 the Nimrod was the subject of a Press conference at Hatfield. The Vice-Chief of the Air Staff, Sir Peter Fletcher, proclaimed: 'Nimrod … is an absolutely brand-new aeroplane!' In fact it would be fairer to describe it as the best that could be done at the time, with the available budget and time-scale. Eventually the MR.2 was to transform its operational capability, while in the new century the MRA.4 offers the hope of making each Nimrod a self-contained air force.

Unfortunately, the MRA.4 programme has failed to adhere to any kind of timetable. This has been partly explained by the extreme difficulty encountered in mating the new wings with the existing fuselages. We are told that the problem is due to the fact that new wings are being constructed using modern computer-based techniques, and are therefore accurate, whereas: 'Nimrod fuselages differ from each other by as much as 4 in' (10 cm). The author simply does not believe this. The 49 Nimrods were all built in precise jigs, at a high rate. The author cannot see how any fuselage could differ in dimensions from its predecessor by more than about ¼ in (6.35 mm). To achieve a discrepancy of 4 in, the operational flying would have had to stress the fuselage beyond its elastic limit, and this again is beyond belief.

Chapter 7

The Nimrod MR.2

At the time of their first flight, all but the simplest aircraft are already out of date. This has never been more sharply in evidence than in the case of the Nimrod. As was emphasised in the preceding chapter, while the Nimrod MR.1 was the best that – in the British political and financial environment – could be done in the available time-scale, it was far from what could be achieved by packaging more modern equipment into the same airframe. This was appreciated even when the Nimrod was in the design stage, and it was accepted as inevitable that the MR.1 aircraft would fairly soon have to be largely gutted, and re-equipped with less-archaic contents.

What was then much less obvious was that, many years later, it would be necessary to remanufacture the entire aircraft, to fit it for possibly an additional 40 years of service, in a world posing totally different challenges. This is now having to be done, in an even more stringent financial environment, as described in the final chapter.

In the 1970s, the principal reason for upgrading the original Nimrod was the transformation of the Soviet Union's submarine fleet. Though the USSR was certainly not an enemy, it was nevertheless considered to pose a serious potential threat, especially to members of the NATO alliance. When the MR.1 aircraft were being delivered, the USSR was rapidly replacing its large fleets of noisy diesel-engined boats by nuclear-powered submarines, which could travel much faster, much deeper and by previous standards, almost noiselessly, to all parts of the world. This was the main driving force in making it essential to package completely new ASW (anti-submarine warfare) equipment into the MR.1 airframes.

The process of upgrading Nimrods to the MR.2 standard began in 1975. At that time it had long been accepted that it was not a practical proposition to transform the entire weapons system from analog to digital, nor to provide a modern flight deck with digital multifunction displays. What could be done, with considerable difficulty and within the limited funding, was to link many of the existing navigation aids and sensors, especially the acoustics, plus several important additions, through three completely new items, all digital: a radar processor, an acoustics processor and a central tactical computer. Among other upgrades was the replacement of the primitive search radar by one of much later basic design. The result not only gives answers faster, but also provided significant new capabilities.

At the risk of boring some readers, many others might welcome a very brief outline of the meaning of analog and digital. As a first step, one can consider two simple calculators. A slide-rule is an analog device, giving a quick approximation. The author's maths professor once showed him what another of his students had written: '68÷17 = 3.98', showing that a slide-rule can be made to give a silly answer. Analog computers *measure*; they operate upon continuous variables, such as an electrical voltage or resistance. In contrast, digital devices *count*, a simple example being an abacus, where you slide beads up and down wires, each bead being a digit to a power of 10. If you inputted the above division sum to a digital computer you could never get any answer other than precisely 4. Today there are many kinds of A/D (analog-to-digital) and D/A converter, and we seem almost to have reached the stage where there is nothing we cannot do, often with a device that can be carried in the pocket.

Obviously, upgrading the Nimrod to MR.2 standard was a major effort. Even then, the result was not even a half-way house to perfection, but it was at least a giant step forward. The Central Tactical System, created by GEC Avionics (previously Marconi Elliott Avionics Systems), was managed by a 920-ATC computer with thousands of times more capacity than the primitive device in the Nimrod MR.1. It transformed both the computing and the display facilities, and combined with a Ferranti inertial navigation system (INS), also the flight-control and navigation. The new radar, called Searchwater, was developed by Thorn-EMI Electronics, and operates in conjunction with a dedicated Ferranti 1600D digital computer and a Thorn-EMI colour display. It was about two generations later in capability than the ASV-21D radar previously fitted, and could distinguish the periscope or snorkel of a submarine at the limit of its operating range. The author was astonished to see the total contrast between the old and new displays, and the automatic processing of IFF reply codes.

As explained above, when the Nimrod MR.2 was being developed, its most important missions were expected to be against hostile submarines. To meet the increased threat, the greatly upgraded Ultra Electronics AQS-901 acoustics processing and display system was centred on its own dedicated pair of 920-ATC computers. This considerably eased the task of the operator, using FFT (fast Fourier transform) processing, in conjunction with all likely active and passive sonobuoys. The latter included the Ultra Electronics Cambs (command active multi-beam sonobuoy), the Anglo-Australian Barra directional passive buoy, the American

This unidentified MR.2 has ground electrical power plugged in, ready for engine start.

SSQ-41 and SSQ-53, and the Canadian Tandem. The AQS-901 system could monitor thirty buoys simultaneously, avoiding mutual interference, and recording everything on multi-track tape for subsequent analysis. Communications were enhanced by adding a duplicate AD.470 h.f. radio, together with a teletype and on-line encryption system.

To reduce expenditure of sonobuoys, a system called ACT.1 (airborne crew trainer) was developed by the GEC Avionics Maritime Aircraft Systems Division. This was centred on a control station based upon a display unit, with push-button inputs, and a magnetic-tape reader. It enabled the AQS-901 processing and display system to operate in a training role, essentially like a computer game, with one crew-member playing the part of an elusive hostile submarine.

The most visible change in the MR.2 was to repaint the entire aircraft in a new NATO-approved khaki-like colour called Hemp, and to switch to B-type plain red/blue national markings. Another visible change was to fit an upgraded APU (auxiliary power unit) and environmental system, behind the rear pressure bulkhead, under the fin. The increased APU airflow required the addition of an external ram-air inlet on the left side, just ahead of the tailplane. Also visible externally was the 'towel-rail' antenna serving the Decca Loran ADL-21 long-range navigation aid, above the fuselage, which many MR.1 aircraft had lacked. Less obvious was the installation of a crucial communications system, TADIL-A Link 11, which gives instantaneous digital contact between all participating stations, in the air, on the ground, or in ships. Not least, by this time the Agiflite camera, mentioned in the preceding chapter, had become standard kit.

Of the forty-six Nimrod MR.1 aircraft, a total of thirty-five were upgraded to MR.2 standard, the first, XV236, being redelivered on 23 August 1979. More than half the Nimrod force had been upgraded when, on 2 April 1982, Argentine forces invaded the Falkland Islands. Exceedingly remote, in the far South Atlantic, this was Sovereign territory, and by chance the United Kingdom had a Prime Minister who never hesitated in deciding that the islands should be returned to British control. Operation Corporate was launched, and decisions were taken in hours, which normally would either have taken years or, probably, would never have been taken at all. These decisions included upgrading as many Nimrods as possible to play a role in the campaign. The biggest problem was the almost impossible distance.

The B-type roundels stand out sharply in this unusual view of one of the first Nimrods, XV238. It is pictured after being upgraded to MR.2 standard, with a flight-refuelling probe. *(Philip Jarrett)*

Painted in Hemp colour, this fully updated Nimrod MR.2, XV235, was one of the first to be fitted with wing-tip pods. *(Philip Jarrett)*

There has never been a greater contrast between an RAF aircraft and its intended replacement than between the Shackleton AEW.2 and the Nimrod AEW.3. Here XZ285, intended to be the first production AEW.3, banks sharply away from predecessor WR690. *(Philip Jarrett)*

A picture of what might have been: Nimrod AEW.3 XV263 is seen painted in hemp, and on test complete with flight-refuelling probe and wingtip pods. *(Philip Jarrett)*

Nimrod MRA.4 PA01, ZZ516, on taxi testing along the Warton runway on 20 September 2005. At that time the aircraft was still unpainted. *(Neville Beckett)*

R.A.F. Form 1256F.

TRANSPORT COMMAND

R. A. F.

To PASSENGERS   PLEASE PASS ROUND

From CAPTAIN.....S/L HARRIS............. Aircraft.........................

Time........16 50........G.M.T. ....Local Time

Our position is........OVER N. COAST FRANCE

Altitude........42000....feet. Temperature........-60........deg. Cent.

Ground Speed.....503........miles per hour.

Our Flight Plan estimated a..............hrs..............mins. Flight.

We are..............hrs..............mins. $\frac{\text{ahead of}}{\text{behind}}$ Schedule.

Our estimated time of arrival at.......................................

is.......................G.M.T. ....Local Time.

In...............mins. we should pass on our $\frac{\text{Starboard}}{\text{Port}}$

.....We intend to arrive.......
.....over Lyneham at 20000.......
.....and then make / rapid.......
                        FAIRLY

Remarks : ....
.....descent.......

.............Andrew.............Navigator.

(*135) Wt. 17513—883 10M Pads 8/50 T.S. 839

This unique document was handed to the author during the Comet C.2 Press flight in June 1956, an occasion recalled in the text.

Built as G–APDS, a Comet 4 for BOAC, this aircraft was sold in February 1969 to the Ministry of Supply, becoming test platform XW626. It is pictured at Hawarden (Chester) on 10 June 1972, still wearing the dorsal fin needed for trials with the Nimrod AEW.3 nose radar (Chapter 9). Soon afterwards it was flown to Bedford and scrapped. *(Paul Tomlin)*

Photographers had a field day at Woodford on 21 October 2001 when RA-82045, an An-124 of Volga-Dniepr Tac-Heavylift, arrived with the fuselage of what had been XV253 and was now 9118M. It had come from Kinloss, where the first three selected MR.2 airframes were dismantled. *(Paul Tomlin)*

Looking darrk in two shades of grey, this Nimrod R.1 is seen from the left, showing the long windowless section of forward fuselage, with six operator consoles on the left side.

XV659 was the first Comet 2 to be completely gutted and rebuilt as a Comet 2R of the RAF. It is seen after transfer from 192 to 51 Sqn., at Wyton. *(Philip Jarrett)*

An unusual view of a Nimrod R.1 arriving at Waddington on 2 July 2009. By this time there was an extra blade aerial underneath. *(Neville Beckett)*

Taken on 9 August 1970, this photograph shows BEA Comet 4B G–ARJK on the apron at Manchester. It became one of the many to serve Dan-Air. *(Paul Tomlin)*

XV236, one of the first batch of Nimrod MR.1s, is seen here on a visit to Woodford on 4 June 1998. It had been the first of the thirty-five Nimrods to be upgraded to MR.2 standard, being redelivered, without an FR probe, on 23 August 1979. *(Neville Beckett)*

Nimrod R.1 XW665 landing at Waddington.

Nimrod MRA.4 ZJ518, the PA02 development aircraft, making the first public flypast with the weapons bay doors open. The location was RAF Waddington, on 28 June 2007. *(Neville Beckett)*

Comet 4C G-ARJN awaiting passengers at Manchester on 10 October 1976. This aircraft was known to cabin crew as 'Juliet Noddy', while G-AYVS was 'Victor Sylvester', a popular dance instructor and band leader. *(Paul Tomlin)*

A unique formation over Waddington on 28 June 2007. The E-3D Sentry leads Nimrod R.1 XW665 and the newly delivered Sentinel R.1 ZJ690 of 5(AC) Sqadron. *(Neville Beckett)*

A rare glimpse inside a Nimrod R.1, looking aft, showing the Comint and Elint crews at work. Nearest is the Elint supervisor, with the silver-haired Comint supervisor beyond him. *(Crown Copywight)*

Night falls over Manchester Ringway on 19 September 1976, but the large fleet of Comets operated by Dan-Air remain acttive and can be photographed on the floodlit apron. *(Paul Tomlin)*

Nimrod, R.1 XW664. The row of dorsal antennas is clearly visible. *(Crown copyright)*

A closer view of XW664, now painted in hemp, and with blade antennas on the empty underwing pylons. In the background is one of Waddington's Sentries.

This close-up of the first MRA.4 development aircraft shows the tiny static cone dangling on its multicore cable, which is attached at the top of the fin. At first stretched along the runway, it lifts quickly on take-off. *(Neville Beckett)*

This Nimrod R.1, the replacement aircraft XV249, was photographed while serving with 51 Sqn. at a 'classified location'. The choice is very narrow! *(US Department of Defense)*

A close formation shot of a Nimrod R.1 of 51 Sqn. The thrust reverser on the outboard engine stands
out clearly.

A sprightly fly-past by a Nimrod R.1 at Waddington on 9 May 2009.

A close-up of the tail of Nimrod MRA.4 ZJ518 shows the light-coloured Gurney flap strip stuck on each side of the rudder trailing edge. This is one of the modifications introduced to cure annoying sinusoidal oscillation in flight. *(Neville Beckett)*

On 4 April 2009 ZJ515, the second Nimrod MRA.4 for RAF service, was virtually complete, and was photographed undergoing cabin pressure tests on the Woodford airfield. The fuselage came from MR.2 XV258. *(Paul Tomlin)*

Another view of Nimrod R.1 XW665 in formation with a Boeing Sentry. The 51 Squadron aircraft proudly bear the unit's goose badge on the dorsal fin.

ZJ514, the first production MRA.4, is seen here at Woodford on 10 September 2009. Later that day it made its first flight, to Air Livery plc at Norwich Airport to be painted. *(Paul Tomlin)*

Nimrod MRA.4 ZJ518 is seen here on 6 August 2009 trailing the static cone, seen as a dot on the end of its barely visible cable. From this aspect the increased size of the jetpipes, compared with previous Nimrods, is obvious. *(Nevelle Beckett)*

An essential early decision was to add a flight-refuelling (FR) probe. The crucial factor here was that a useful number of apparently restorable probes already existed, lying around as scrap – one of them in Canada – after being removed from Vulcan bombers. In a matter of hours, Flight Refuelling Ltd, at Tarrant Rushton, in Dorset, had schemed a way to fit a probe, and then link it to the Nimrod's internal tankage. It increased mission endurance from around 12 hours to at least 19 hours. The long probe was mounted at the top of the fuselage on the dorsal centreline, and braced by an inverted-V strut above the cockpit. In order to give the Nimrod pilots a clear view of each contact, the probes were extended in length to project well ahead of the nose, increasing the aircraft's overall length to 129 ft 1 in (39.35 m). In eighteen days the new FR installation was designed, made, tested, certificated, and installed on eight aircraft, closely followed by a further eight. To counter a reduction in yaw (directional) stability, small swept finlets were added above and below the tailplanes, and a small ventral fin was added under the rear fuselage. For several years the probed aircraft were distinguished by the designation MR.2P, the P being removed when probes became standard on all Nimrods. Of course, had funding been available, new probes would have been fitted from the outset.

Other changes included the fitting of weapon-bay racks for bombs or Sting Ray torpedoes, the attachment of launchers to the previously unused underwing hardpoints, to carry either a Harpoon cruise missile or a pair of Sidewinder air-to-air missiles, and the addition of a row of eleven vortex generators above the leading edge of each outer wing. Whether MR.2 Nimrods played a direct role in Operation Corporate has not been revealed, but the next chapter explores the Nimrod R.1's participation.

From 1985 the MR.2 fleet were fitted with an ESM (electronic support measures) pod on each wingtip. Originally produced for the Nimrod R.1, these were made by the Brough, East Yorkshire, factory of British Aerospace, which has ever since played a role in Nimrod programmes. Each pod houses a Loral Electronics 1017 system, with the British designation of ARI. (aeronautical radio installation) 18240/1, and the common code name Yellow Knife. Each wing-tip installation operates through four large spiral antennas, and four small ones. The large antennas are low-band cavity-backed planar spirals, while the small ones are high-band conical spirals. Each of the sixteen antennas offers complete coverage over an azimuth sweep of 90 degrees, and together the coverage extends in all directions,

XV254 is seen here after being brought up to MR.2P standard, with an in-flight refuelling probe. A Sidewinder can be seen on the starboard store pylon. (*Philip Jarrett*)

over a bandwidth of from 2 to 20 GHz. The pods are linked to the tactical system through a dedicated UYS-503 data processor, a product of General Dynamics Canada. Adding the pods required an increase in the size of the yaw-stabilising fins above and below each tailplane.

Operation Desert Storm, unleashed over Iraq from August 1990, resulted in a detachment of six aircraft from Nos.120 (lead), 42 and 206 Sqns. being based from early-1971 at Seeb, in Oman. These were the first Nimrods to be fitted with a Wescam MX-15 electro-optical (EO) power-driven turret, supplied by L-3 Communications. Mounted in a pod carried under the right wing pylon, the turret provides day/night video coverage of the entire hemisphere beneath the aircraft. Other additions to the Desert Storm force included Saab BOZ electronic-countermeasures (ECM) dispenser pods, usually carried on the corresponding attachment under the left wing, and a towed radar decoy streamed behind the aircraft from a compartment in the rear fuselage. Unofficially, these aircraft were dubbed MR.2P(GM), meaning Gulf Modification.

XV249, the 24th Nimrod, is seen about to land at an Open Day at RAF Coningsby on 15 June 1985. It has no probe, but is fitted with Yellow Knife pods on the wingtips. (*Philip Jarrett*)

In 2006 Project Broadsword added the ability to transmit MX-15 imagery to ground stations, and commanders of air and surface forces. Another recent addition, made necessary by the unforeseen need to operate at very low altitudes over hostile terrain, is to fit a new EW (electronic warfare) management system, the ALQ-213. Originally developed for the F-16 fighter, by the Danish contractor Terma, it replaces six or seven cockpit interfaces by four new ones: the EW prime indicator, EW management unit, RWR (radar-warning receiver) azimuth indicator, and tactical-threat display. This is linked with an MCP-10 (modular countermeasures pod) which can be carried on either or both wing pylons. The pod houses a seven-tube magazine, which can be loaded with chaff cartridges, decoy flares, RF warning/jamming antennas, or missile warners.

Another upgrade, not announced at the time, and developed principally for the future Nimrod MRA.4, is to fit the Ultra MSA (multi-static active) capability, in support of the WASP (wide-area search programme). In September 2007

Ultra Electronics Sonar and Communications Systems were cleared to disclose brief details of the demonstration programme, which was carried out with a Nimrod MR.2, on behalf of the Nimrod Integrated Project Team. The original MSA system was based on the following items: Ultra's SSQ-926 Alfea (active low-frequency electro-acoustic) sonobuoy, SSQ-965 Hidar (high dynamic range Difar [directional acoustic frequency analysis and recording]) and SSQ-981E Barra passive buoys, as well as the new General Dynamics Canada AQS-971 acoustic processor, featuring a specific software upgrade to permit multi-static operations. The WASP-equipped MR.2 trials aircraft was in 2008 being evaluated against conventional and nuclear submarines, with a Main Gate report due in 2009.

Towards the end of the 20th Century, despite warfare in countries in the Middle East, and the growth of piracy in important maritime areas, crippling lack of money caused the Nimrod force to be progressively whittled down, until by 2003 it comprised just 42R, 120 and 201 Sqns. Again to save money, all three are now based at Kinloss, with central servicing for all units.

By late-2006, five Nimrod MR.2 aircraft had been lost. On 17 November 1980 a severe birdstrike near Kinloss caused the aircraft eventually to crash, the two pilots being killed. On 3 June 1984 XV257 suffered an unexplained fire in the weapons bay, where the practice flares were located; the crew managed to land, and quickly evacuate, but the aircraft was a total loss. On 16 May 1995 an emergency landing was made at Lossiemouth, close to Kinloss, with one engine on fire, the damage resulting in the aircraft being judged a write-off. On 2 September 1995 the pilots lost control during an air display at Toronto, the aircraft diving fatally into Lake Ontario. On 2 September 2006 XV230 caught fire, and crashed near Kandahar, Afghanistan, during an operational sortie, killing the crew of ten, a marine and an infantryman. In November 2007 a Nimrod made an emergency landing after suffering a fuel leak, which immediately followed an in-flight refuelling. On this occasion there was no fire, but in-flight refuelling of Nimrods was at once discontinued.

The XV230 accident report could only suggest that, about 90 seconds after completing an in-flight refuelling, overflowing fuel somehow escaped and reached No.7 tank dry bay in the right wing root. Here it came into contact with the cross-feed pipe for the Supplementary Conditioning Pack, which, at 400°C, is hot enough to ignite kerosene. Of course, the pipe was lagged, but could have been locally exposed at a joint in the ancient asbestos-type lagging, a shocking admission. Once started there, a fire could not be extinguished. No fewer than thirty-three modifications, most trivial, were triggered by this event.

Though not identified as the cause of XV230's in-flight fire, there has also been concern over leakage of fuel, rather than mere seepage, from the 'tired' integral tanks. More specifically, the loss of XV230 triggered a long-overdue detailed survey of the MR.2 fleet by Qinetiq, the successor company to British Aerospace. By mid-2008 this had revealed a number of places where the long and arduous usage had caused deterioration. Of these, by far the most serious is progressive misalignment of the major fuel pipes along the roof of the weapons bay, putting a severe strain on the supposed fuel-tight joints. This problem emerged into the public arena after May 2008, when the coroner handling the XV230 post-mortems demanded that the 'unsafe' Nimrods should be grounded. This triggered an angry response by the Ministry, while in the background feverish activity was seeking the best way to make the Nimrods safe, if possible without spending much money.

Perhaps inevitably, the official inquiry into the loss of XV230 threw up various irregularities, and tended to magnify seemingly unimportant acts. Sqn Ldr Guy Bazalgette, Commander of the Afghanistan Nimrod detachment, publicly apologised for having shredded various XV230 documents, while emphasising that they could not have had any bearing on the inquiry. More significant was the fact that Charles Haddon-Cave, the QC heading the Inquiry, sent so-called 'Salmon letters' to senior officers and various organisations warning them that they were 'likely to be criticised' in his findings – due to be published in July or August 2009 – and giving them time to formulate their responses.

It was a straightforward task to redesign the lethal hot-air duct, modify the sealing throughout the fuel system and ensure that fire could not break out in a bay devoid of protection. Priority was naturally given to the R.1 aircraft, all of which were returned to service fairly quickly in what is considered to be a safe condition. By March 2009 three Nimrod MR.2s had also been modified, but – fearing a second disaster – it was then announced that from 31 March, the remaining twelve MR.2s would at last be grounded. Bob Ainsworth, Minister of State for the Armed forces, said: 'This will free up the maximum number of aircraft for the modification programme'. He added, vaguely, that it was hoped to have the fleet flying again 'by the summer'.

By September 2009 eight of the eleven active MR.2s had had all the immediately required modifications incorporated, while a further three were in deep maintenance at Kinloss. This enables the RAF to sustain two aircraft, each with two crews, on overseas deployment – presumably back in Afghanistan – until the last MR.2 is withdrawn from service. Final withdrawal is still scheduled for 2011, but the past record suggests the real date will be up to a year later.

Fortunately, in the next-generation Nimrod MRA.4 all the suspect items are removed, or completely rebuilt. However, before describing the MRA.4 it is necessary to turn to two totally different kinds of Nimrod. The Nimrod AEW.3 was a strikingly modified aircraft, which had the lethal misfortune to be developed for customers who, incapable of fairly assessing the situation themselves, were mesmerised by an American alternative, just as has happened to British programmes many times in the past.

In contrast, the Nimrod R.1 has had the great good fortune to be so secretive that, until recently, it has not attracted the attention of politicians. Instead, it has been able to get on with the job, flying real missions in real wars that no other aircraft in the world could accomplish. Even here, however, moves are now afoot to replace it by an equally geriatric American aircraft, matched to American missions.

Chapter 8

The Nimrod R.1

This chapter is unique. It is the only one in the author's 383 books to have been based almost entirely on research by another writer. This is because that writer, Jon Lake, has conducted diligent and prolonged research into the story of Britain's most secret aircraft, the Nimrod R.1. Jon reported his findings in two issues of *Air International*, July 2001 and April 2008. The author therefore also acknowledges a debt to that periodical's former Editor, Malcolm English.

In Chapter 4 it was explained how, on 21 August 1958, No.192 Sqn. of the Royal Air Force was renumbered as 51 Sqn., though it continued to be based at Watton, Norfolk, as an element of Signals Command. Its mission was to fly often quite dangerous missions gathering Sigint, Elint and Comint. In 1963 the squadron was transferred to Bomber (later called Strike) Command, and moved to Wyton, which was then in Huntingdon, and is now in Cambridgeshire. Here the unit – which never officially existed as part of Wyton's establishment – operated Comet R.1 aircraft until these were replaced by three special Nimrods, which were designated as R.1s. In 1995 No.51 Sqn. moved to Waddington, Lincolnshire, where it remains at the time of writing, one of its Nimrods having been lost, and later replaced.

Visibly, these aircraft can be identified by having a thimble-like antenna on the front of each pinion tank, and a third identical thimble on the extreme tail, replacing the long MAD boom of the Nimrod MR.2. Each aircraft also has a flying goose, 51's badge, painted in red on the dorsal fin.

It is fair to describe 51 Sqn. as the most secretive unit in the RAF. Brief published histories of the unit state that the Nimrod R.1s replaced the Comets from 1972, August 1973, December 1973 and May 1974. In fact, deliveries of the special Nimrods to 51 Sqn. actually began in July 1971, but at that time they were almost devoid of what might be termed mission equipment. Installing everything, wiring it up, and checking it out, took almost three years.

It was certainly not a case of just transferring the items from the Comets to the Nimrods. The Nimrod R.1 started life with the best array of electronic eavesdropping and recording equipment that the parsimonious Treasury could afford, and many additional or replacement items have been added since. Indeed, because of the exceptional priority accorded to these aircraft, they have been updated with unusual frequency – approximately once per year – and this makes a detailed description even more difficult.

The basic mission of an intelligence-gathering aircraft is to listen to emissions or signals of possible interest, to identify them, and record them if necessary. Sigint (signals intelligence) consists basically of Elint (electronic intelligence) and Comint (communications intelligence), but there are other branches such as Radint (radiation intelligence), the study of emissions which appear not to convey any information. In time of conflict, or other military operations, it may be necessary to interfere with these signals, either by jamming (swamping them with noise), or by re-broadcasting them after a short or variable time-delay, or in a cunningly altered form.

So far as is known publicly, all such operations normally require a direct line of sight, from the aircraft to the source of the signal. Moreover, the source is probably on the ground, and either motionless or moving very slowly, compared to the speed of the aircraft. Therefore, to keep this line of sight unbroken, possibly over long periods, the aircraft has to fly in a circle, or a racetrack pattern, or figure-8. The task is further complicated by the obvious fact that a precisely repeated orbit, in hostile airspace, could be inviting disaster. Flying a pattern requires an angle of bank, and these factors determine the best positions on the aircraft for the receiver antennas, to keep reception at the best level without any part of the aircraft getting in the way.

It follows that the Nimrod R.1 has antennas distributed along the top and bottom of the fuselage, on the fin, and, most obviously on the extreme tail and on the so-called 'pinion tanks' projecting ahead of the wings. What is much less evident is that the largest and possibly the most important antennas are under the cabin floor, in what in other Nimrods is the weapons bay. It would have been an advantage from several points of view, if the under-floor area could have been included in the pressurised and air-conditioned structure, but time and the budget militated against this. At least the Nimrod R.1's main cabin is pressurised, unlike that of its predecessor, the Comet R.1.

Instead, the former weapons bay has been provided with improved heating and ventilation, and fitted to house a large removable pannier. It is fair to assume that, in contrast to the light alloy weapons-bay doors and under-skin around the lower part of the MR Nimrods, the corresponding doors of the R.1, ahead of the wings and below cabin-floor level, are made of dielectric material, probably a special glass-fibre. These doors must be transparent to electronic wavelengths and cause no distortion.

On the pannier are four bays, housing the principal row of receiver antennas, each of which is a power-driven dish looking out to left or right, or both. At the start of fitting equipment into the Nimrod R.1s, Hawker Siddeley provided the rigid pannier structure, incorporating hydraulically driven pedestals on which are normally mounted the antennas. Each antenna is probably an inverse-Cassegrain (paraboloid reflector) dish. These antennas are colloquially called spinners, doubtless because they rotate on a vertical axis. Situated at the front, Bay 1 houses the largest, a Ferranti dish, 5 ft (1,524 mm) across, almost filling the under-floor space. Bay 2 houses three similar spinners, each with a 33 in (838 mm) dish, Bay 3 can accommodate two 26 in (660 mm) dishes, and Bay 4 houses a single dish measuring 15 in (381 mm). In addition, a 'special' spiral antenna, the geometry of which must be planar, is housed in the dorsal fin, which is in consequence slightly extended in area. All the spinners are precisely stabilised, ignoring manoeuvres of the aircraft.

Geometrically similar spinners are also mounted on stabilised platforms attached to the front bulkhead of each wing pinion tank, and a third is mounted on Frame 54, the final fuselage frame at the tail, which in MR Nimrods carries the MAD boom. These three antennas each have a diameter of 20 in (508 mm), and sweep over an azimuth arc of precisely 180 degrees. What is rather remarkable is that, though it is vital to 'see' as clearly as possible, the hemispherical radomes over these three antennas have been repeatedly painted. Initially, when the aircraft were painted in standard white, with grey undersides, these radomes were black. Later, when the aircraft were repainted in hemp, the radomes became brownish yellow. From April 2001, the hemp was replaced by pale sea grey, and this finish colour now also covers the wing radomes, that on the tail – at the time of writing – remaining yellow.

The normal flight crew originally comprised two pilots, with a flight engineer immediately behind them, and in the forward main cabin on the left side, two navigators, whose task was often to position the aircraft with extremely high precision, 'in the middle of nowhere', where there would be little in the way of surface navigation aids. In 1980 the Searchwater nose radar, as fitted to the Nimrod MR.2, was replaced by an Ekco.290, with the display in the cockpit and viewed by the pilots. Thus, on most missions, the need for a radar navigator was eliminated. Together with the lighter weight of the radar, this balances the mass of the row of spinners. A folding door normally separates the flight deck from the main tactical compartment.

Here, the mission crew, comprised of highly skilled Comint and Elint special-ists, are distributed in closely spaced rows to left or right, all facing outwards except for three Comint specialists who face forwards. Originally there were to be stations for up to twenty-three electronics specialists, but in fact the number needed has grown with the workload, and is now up to thirty-three. Normal stations for a Nimrod R.1 crew are depicted in Mike Badrocke's cutaway, and in the cabin plan view by Rolando Ugolini, of Key Publishing. As the mission-crew numbers have increased, so has the extra equipment caused three of the left-hand cabin windows to be blanked off, reducing the number of side windows to five.

The two drawings show the location of the main equipment consoles, all of them side-facing, which are the interface between the specialist crew and the mission. Consoles 1–5 are on the left, in the front compartment ahead of the main-spar, Frame 27. Consoles 6–13 are on the right, in the rear compartment behind, Frame 29. The drawings show a normal division of these stations to handle Comint, Sigint and Elint functions. If necessary, two or more operators can attend to the analysis and recording of a single signal. Certain special Comint tasks are handled by the three dedicated operators – who might be fluent in a foreign language – sitting at the individual consoles, facing forwards.

As originally completed, the R.1 had a basic avionics suite comprising AD.360 ADF, AD.260 VOR/ILS, ARN-172 Tacan, ARA-50 u.h.f./d.f., dual ADL-21 Loran C/A. Because of the need to establish precise position in remote regions, a further item is a Kollsman periscopic sextant. As previously noted, the original radar was replaced by an Ekco product, which eliminated the need for a separate radar operator. At one of the frequent upgrades a (possibly previously used by a civil airliner) ASN-119 Carousel IVA INS (inertial navigation system) was installed, enabling one Loran navigation aid to be removed, together with the left-hand 'towel-rail' antenna above the fuselage.

The first R.1 to contain all its special equipment, XW664, began flight testing at Wyton on 21 October 1973. Operational flying started on 3 May 1974. The remaining aircraft, '65 and '66, became operational later in 1974. On 8 April 1976 a standard Nimrod MR.1, XZ283, was supplied to 51 Sqn. to assist in training R.1 pilots. The R.1 trio themselves could not be spared for such flying, and replacing the co-pilot by a pupil on operational missions was not thought to be a good idea. XZ283 was later converted into an AEW.3.

In the 1980s the R.1 suite of antennas was augmented by the addition of aft-facing 'hockey-stick' antennas above and below each tailplane, and above and below each wing pinion tank, while three were added above the forward fuselage. The wide spacing of these antennas increases accuracy when measuring small differences in TOA (time of arrival), in order to pinpoint an emitter's precise location. Additional antennas are almost certainly housed in the 'rugby ball' fairing on top of the fin, which in MR Nimrods houses ESM equipment. This would appear to be the obvious place for a Satcom (satellite communications) antenna.

On 4 March 1982 the sudden panic to recapture the Falkland Islands resulted in disruption to the R.1 force. The navigators were diverted into teaching their counterparts in Vulcans and Victors how to use the complex Carousel inertial systems, which had been hastily stripped out from retired VC10s, while the aircraft themselves were fitted with in-flight refuelling probes in the manner described in Chapter 7. Aircraft '64, at least, was able to play an active role in the operation. After the conflict, No.51 Sqn. proudly added 'South Atlantic' to the battle honours on its standard, but how it operated, and from which airfield(s), has yet to be disclosed.

The three R.1s were the first Nimrods to be fitted with ESM pods on the wing tips. As described in Chapter 7, these quite large installations were made by British Aerospace at Brough, and contain an array of receivers served by four large and four small high- and low-band antennas. The crucial electronics were supplied by Loral Electronics but as the actual antenna installation in the Nimrod R.1 is quite different from that in the MR.2 – in ways yet to be revealed – the system has the code name Yellow Gate, not Yellow Knife.

In August 1990, No. 51 Sqn. became based on an unidentified airfield in support of operations over Kuwait and Iraq, remaining there until March 1992. As already noted, in April 1995 the squadron moved from Wyton to Waddington. Three weeks later, on 16 May, XW666 lived up to its ominous serial number. On test after a period of maintenance, with seven people on board, it suffered 'a catastrophic engine fire'. Perhaps the most serious disadvantage to buried engine installations is that any serious, or sustained, engine fire is almost certain to weaken the crucial primary structure of the wing, especially the spars and any other spanwise members. On this occasion, wing failure was considered to be seconds away, rather than minutes. The captain, Flt Lt Art Stacey, pulled off a masterly wheels-up ditching in the Moray Firth, earning an Air Force Cross. Arguably, this was the first successful ditching by any four-jet aircraft, and it almost certainly would have been catastrophic with under-wing engines. There were no crew injuries and the crushed nose of 666 is today on view at RAF Finningley, Doncaster.

Despite the carnage following the Nimrod AEW.3 debacle, the run-down of the Nimrod squadrons meant that several surplus airframes were still available to replace 666. The vital importance of the R.1 aircraft meant that decisions were astonishingly quick. Following a survey, XV249 was selected, and on 23 June 1995, barely a month after the loss of 666, BAe Aerospace Defence was faxed a hastily drafted contract, a total of £30 million having been made available. Following a major overhaul, XV249 was ferried to Woodford, on 23 October 1995. After conversion to a basic R.1 airframe, it was flown to Waddington on 19 December 1996 for 'stuffing' (installing the mission systems and equipment).

Jon Lake takes up the story:

At the time that XW666 was lost, 51 Squadron's Nimrods were being extensively modernised under the *Starwindow* programme. This had been launched to meet a September 1991 requirement, and a contract had been awarded to E-Systems Melpar Division to design and supply a new Open Systems architecture digital Sigint suite. Probably derived from the equipment carried by USAF Boeing RC-135V Rivet Joint aircraft, the *Starwindow* system incorporated two 'operationally proven' high-speed search receivers, a wide-band digital direction-finding system, and 22 pooled digital

The crushed nose of XW666 at RAF Finningley.

intercept receivers (probably Raytheon Systems Nanomin). New workstations were added, with colour active-matrix liquid-crystal displays, distributed digital maps, data-bases and analytical tools. *Starwindow* also included three types of ground-data analysis system (GAS) facilities, fixed and mobile. The primary GAS was capable of exploiting data which could be data-linked from the airborne Nimrod, while Alternative and Tactical GASs were also provided, together with a new crew-training system.

Starwindow had been planned for installation between April 1994 and October 1995, following factory testing. Flight-testing of the core *Starwindow* suite began during August 1994, and two aircraft are believed to have been upgraded when 666 was lost ... The Electronic Warfare and Electronics Detachment at Waddington began work on XV249 on 27 December 1996, *Starwindow* being installed from 10 January ... The aircraft began ground calibration on 21 March, and flew as an R.1 on 11 April. Conversion from an MR.2 had taken 56,583 man-hours. A further upgrade, Project Extract, would have matched the R.1 to RAF skills and proce-dures, but was cancelled on grounds of cost.

Inevitably, 51 Sqn. played a crucial role in Operation Desert Fox in December 1998, and through the 1990s over former Yugoslavia, whilst continuing to fulfil a vital role over the Gulf. For Operation Iraqi Freedom the main operating base was Prince Sultan, in Saudi Arabia. The principal focus of operations then shifted to Afghanistan. *The Sunday Times* revealed that, on 26 December 2006, an R.1 was used to detect and then track the satellite telephone of Mullah Akhtar Mohammed Osmani, the Taliban Treasurer and one pillar of the leadership triad. The Nimrod called in a US aircraft, which placed a GPS-guided bomb directly on the Mullah's 4 × 4.

Making a break with the tradition of secrecy, on 3 April 2007, the American company L-3 Communication:

> announced today that its Integrated Sytems subsidiary has been selected to receive a contract worth more than £11.5 million ($21.7 million) from the UK MoD. Upon Main Gate approval, expected in June 2009, L-3 will be the preferred contractor to execute the Project Helix Demonstration and Manufacture contract, which has a projected value of up to £400 million ($756 million) over a 7-year period, with the first aircraft delivery scheduled in early 2013…
>
> L-3, the lead systems integrator and prime contractor, heads a team that includes QinetiQ, LogicaCMG and BAE Systems Integrated Systems Technologies. QineticQ will provide electronic-reconnaissance technologies, and LogicaCMG will contribute ground systems, information management, and security services and technologies. BAE Systems will provide aircraft modification and certification, long-term support and logistics services, and some sensor technologies … The modification will be performed at RAF Waddington, with final integration and flight testing conducted at Greenville, Texas.

This is great news, because it would not have been practical without a careful survey of the R.1 aircraft to ensure their future life-expectancy. The L-3 contract, which clearly will be vital to the continued life of the R.1 force, should enable these unique aircraft to continue to build on their enviable reputation – the US intelligence fraternity calls them the 'Gift Horse' – until after 2025. Through most of this time they are expected to operate alongside Boeing RC-135U Combat Sent Elint platforms and RC-135V/W Rivet Joint Comint platforms. Though even older than the Nimrods, these are more capacious aircraft, and for several years the omnipotent 'switch to American' lobby in the British Treasury and RAF have tried to get the three Nimrod R.1s either augmented or replaced by RC-135s. On 2 October 2008 they succeeded, with the following announcement:

> The Defense Security Cooperation Agency notified Congress today of a possible Foreign Military Sale requested by the United Kingdom, to convert three USAF KC-135R aircraft into RC-135V/W Rivet Joint aircraft, as well as three APX-119 IFF systems, three LN-100GT inertial reference units, five JTIDS terminals, 18 ABC-210 radios, and 28 ABC-210 radio control heads, modification kits, integration and installation, a ground distributed processing station, modular processing system, airborne capability-extension system, mission trainer, tools and test equipment, spare and repair parts, publications, personnel training and training equipment, support equipment, US Government and contractor representative technical and logistics personnel service, and other related elements of logistics support. The total value … could be as high as $1.068 billion.

In a nutshell, the Nimrod R.1 has, predictably, done an enormous job with only just adequate resources, and certainly an inadequate number of aircraft. For many years these constantly overworked aircraft have been almost 'bursting at the seams', and in fact it would have been better if the Nimrod R.1 fuselages had remained at the same length as the Comet 4C, as would have been possible at the outset. For the longer term, the best solution might be to package the future R.1 system into an airframe based on the Nimrod MRA.4, but that appears to be a forlorn hope, especially as so much scarce defence money will now be channelled into the Rivet Joint aircraft.

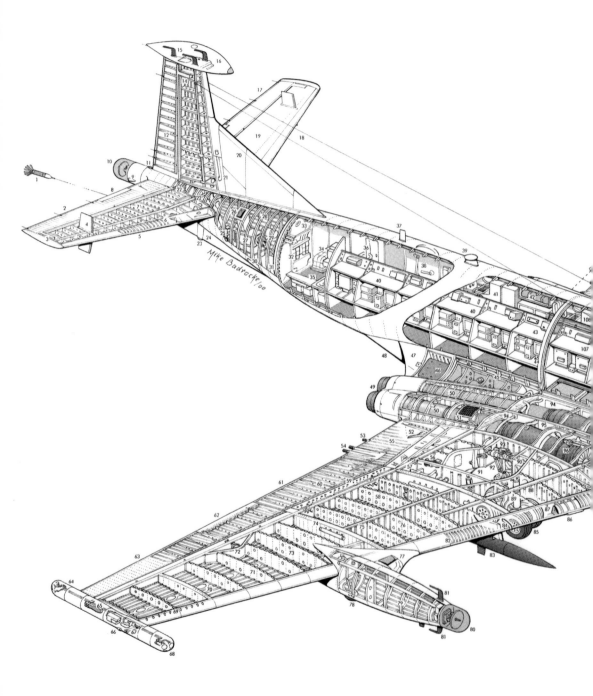

Mike Badrocke/00

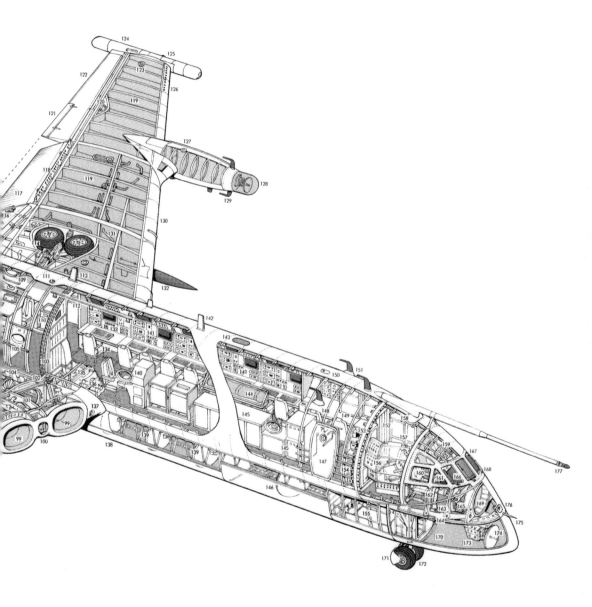

British Aerospace Nimrod R.1, cutaway drawing key

1. Towed radar decoy (TRD)
2 Starboard elevator
3 Aileron mass balance
4 Tailplane auxiliary fins, above and below
5 Leading edge thermal de-icing
6 TRD housing
7 Tailplane rib structure
8 Elevator tab
9 Rear RWR antenna, port and starboard
10 Tail radome housing 20-in Ferranti 'Spinner' antenna
11 Tail navigation light
12 Rudder rib structure
13 Fin rib structure
14 Rudder mass balance
15 Aft D/F (voice) antennae
16 Fin tip antenna fairing
17 Port elevator
18 HF antenna cables
19 Port tailplane
20 Extended fin root fairing housing 'special' spiral antenna
21 Fin de-icing air duct
22 Fin and tailplane spar mounting bulkheads
23 Tail bumper
24 Ventral fin
25 Auxiliary Power Unit (APU) intake
26 APU exhaust
27 APU in fireproof housing
28 Tailcone frame and stringer structure
29 APU oil tank
30 Tailcone access hatch
31 Rear pressure dome
32 Equipment cooling air ducting
33 Cabin pressurization valves
34 Crew baggage stowage
35 Galley compartment
36 Port side toilet compartment
37 Rear Communications antenna
38 Rear entry door
39 SATCOM antenna
40 Electronic intelligence (ELINT) and Communications intelligence (Coms/Int) operator consoles
41 Auxiliary station 'C'
42 Life jacket stowage
43 Coms/Int supervisor's console
44 Rear spar attachment fuselage main frame
45 Wing root fuel tank

46 Life raft stowage, port and starboard
47 Wing root trailing edge fairing
48 Ventral pannier aft fairing
49 Engine exhaust nozzles
50 Jet pipes, canted outboard
51 Thrust reverser cascade, above and below outboard engines only
52 Spilit trailing edge flap beneath exhaust ducts, down position
53 Fuel vent outlet
54 Fuel dump nozzles
55 Inboard plain flap segment
56 Flap hydraulic jack
57 Rear spar
58 Wing panel inboard integral fuel tankage, total system capacity 48.778-lit (10,730-Imp gal)
59 Starboard airbrake panels, above and below, hydraulically actuated
60 Flap panel rib structure
61 Outboard plain flap segment
62 Aileron tab
63 Starboard aileron
64 Wing tip ESM pod
65 Internal aileron mass balance
66 Starboard navigation light
67 Wing de-icing air spill duct
68 ESM antennae, fore and aft
69 Vortex generators
70 Wing bottom skin/stringer panel with manhole access hatches
71 Outer wing panel rib structure
72 Aileron actuating linkage
73 Outboard integral fuel tankage
74 Outer wing panel joint rib
75 Auxiliary spar
76 Inboard wing rib structure
77 Slotted external tank fairing
78 External tank protective bumper
79 Fixed external fuel tank
80 Starboard radome housing 20-in Ferranti 'Spinner' antenna
81 D/F (voice) antennae, above and below
82 Leading edge corrugated inner skin de-icing air ducts
83 BOZ chaff/flare pod
84 Leading edeg fence
85 Starboard main undercarriage four-wheel bogie

86 Leading edeg stall strip
87 De-icing air supply duct
88 Wing main spar
89 Main undercarriage shock absorber strut
90 Pressure refuelling panel
91 Mainwheel bay
92 Side breaker strut and retraction linkage
93 Hydraulic retraction jack
94 Starboard engine bays
95 Engine bay dividing firewall
96 Rolls-Royce RB168-20 Spey 250 turbofan engines
97 Intake ducting
98 Landing light
99 Starboard engine air intakes
100 Heat exchanger air intake
101 Starboard air conditioning pack
102 Main spar/fuselage attachment joint
103 Fuselage main bulkhead
104 Wing panel centre-section spar box
105 Starboard emergency escape hatch
106 Centre-section bag-type fuel tanks
107 ELINT supervisor's consoles
108 Auxiliary startion 'B'
109 Port emergency escape hatches (2)
110 Recording equipment racks
l11 Upper anti-collision beacon
112 LORAN 'towel rail' antenna
113 Communications antenna
114 Port main undercarriage, stowed position
115 Port inboard flap, down position
116 Flap interconecting link
117 Outboard flap panel, down position
118 Airbrake panel extended, upper and lower surfaces
119 Port wing integral fuel tankage
120 Aileron control linkage
121 Aileron trim tab
122 Port aileron
123 Over fuel filler, three positions
124 Port wing tip ESM pod
125 Port navigation light
126 Vortex generators
127 Fixed external fuel tank
128 Port radome housing 20-in Ferranti 'Spinner' antenna
129 D/F (voice) antennae
130 Thermally de-iced leading edge
131 Fuel system piping
132 Port BOZ chaff/flare launching pod
133 Forward cabin ELINT console
134 Side facing operator's seats
135 Underfloor conditioned air ducting
136 Hydraulic equipment bay
137 Wing root fairing with taxying light
138 Hinged di-electric panels, replacing weapons bay doors of MR. Mk 1 varians
139 Tripple 33-in Ferranti 'Spinner' antennae, two 26-in and one 15-in antennae in aft bays
140 Auxiliary station 'A'
141 Combined consoles, LH ELINT and RH Coms/Int
142 VHF/UHF antenna
143 ADF antenna
144 Life jacket stowage
145 Equipment cabinets
146 Forward scanner bay housing 5-ft Ferranti 'Spinner' antenna
147 Forward entry door
148 Navigator's station
149 Spare Navigator's seat
150 Sextant aperture
151 Forward D/F (voice) antennae
152 Screened cockpit doorway
153 Cockpit section structural bulkhead
154 Starboard systems equipment crate
155 Nosewheel bay with internally opening doors
156 Flight Engineer's station
157 Port. systems equipment crates
158 Cockpit roof escape hatch, inoperative with refuelling boom fitted
159 Overhead switch panel
160 Two-Pilot cockpit layout
161 Direct vision opening side window panel
162 Control column
163 Pitot head, port and starboard
164 Artificial feel system pressure head
165 Rudder pedals
166 Shrouded instrument console
167 Electrically heated windscreen panels
168 Windscreen wipers
169 Front pressure bulkhead
170 Nose conpartment radome
171 Nosewheel fixed mudguard
172 Twin nosewheels, aft retracting
173 Scanner mounting
174 Ekco 290 radar scanner
175 Stand-by pitot head
176 Taxying light
177 Fixed flight refuelling probe

Chapter 9

The Nimrod AEW.3

In this narrative, British Treasury parsimony has figured repeatedly, and it is difficult to find a better example of this than to study the history of APS-20. In 1941 things were very different. Britain was then a world leader in technology, and it did an astonishing deal with the United States which gave that country two new British developments of the very greatest importance, which were previously secret. One was the turbojet. The other was radar, working at centimetric wavelengths.

Such radar had been made possible by the magnetron electronic valve, which had been invented by the University of Birmingham and the General Electric Company (GEC), at Wembley, Middlesex. By 1943 a totally different General Electric company, GE in the USA, had teamed with the Massachusetts Institute of Technology (MIT) to create the world's first airborne radar able to look down over a vast area of the Earth's surface. By 1944 this had become APS-20, already in action in the Pacific, taken aloft by extremely pregnant-looking Grumman Avengers. By 1953 similar radars, fitted to Douglas AD-4W Skyraiders, were serving with Britain's Fleet Air Arm. The same installations were then transferred to Westland (ex-Fairey) Gannet AEW.3 aircraft, and finally, as the APS-20(F), between 1971 and 1974 the same radars were installed in the RAF's twelve Shackleton AEW.2s, to provide Britain with an aerial surveillance fleet. By this time, despite minor updating, the ancient radars were not exactly state of the art.

An early artwork of the AEW.3.

In the Shackletons the sheer skill of the operators went some way to making up for the prehistoric equipment, but they could not contravene the laws of nature. One of these laws was that APS-20 was almost useless against a fast target coming in at tree top height. On the other hand, in 1958 GE reported to the US Navy that it could make a radar that combined u.h.f. (ultra-high frequency) wavelengths with AMTI (airborne moving-target indication), which would solve the problem. By this time, fleets of bombers designed for high altitude, such as the British V-bombers and the USAF B-52, were being hastily modified to attack as close to the ground as possible. The USSR was doing the same. Thus, it was common sense to consider AEW aircraft that could defend against such threats.

By 1964, AMTI radars were competing with those using an even newer system, FMICW (frequency-modulated independent carrier-wave). Within a year, project designers in many companies were sketching aircraft carrying new kinds of large and powerful surveillance radar. Some had the scanner rotating inside a giant discus-shape carried on a pylon above the fuselage. Others made the discus shape become the antenna itself, rotating on its pylon. By far the most important of these was the APS-125, with a 24 ft (7.3 m) disc rotating at 5 or 6 rpm above a Grumman E-2 Hawkeye (an amazing exercise in packaging the radar and crew of five into a small carrier-based airframe). Other schemes had an elliptical dish underneath the fuselage. These looked strange, and so did the FASS (fore-and-aft scanner system), with an inverted-Cassegrain (paraboloid reflector) antenna inside a grossly bulged nose, and a second on the tail, each sweeping in precise succession through 180 degrees to give perfect all-round coverage. Many and varied were the AEW proposals of this period, in the mid-1960s. The British ones are recorded in the book *Airborne Early Warning* by Mike Hirst, published in 1983. Since then, not a great deal of progress has been made; or at least, not a lot has been made public.

Hirst tells in detail the prolonged and sorry saga of how brilliant British designs were repeatedly thwarted by the Treasury. Time and again, the people who knew what they were doing were either simply stopped, or else told to do something different. He relates how, at an advanced stage, with much of the design completed, it was suddenly decreed that a carrier-based AEW aircraft was no longer needed, and the work was halted. After all, Argentina would never think of invading the Falklands, would they? The result was the loss of several almost defenceless British ships, one a vital merchant vessel and the others modern warships.

The obvious platform for a land-based AEW aircraft was the Nimrod. Mike goes on to describe the different forms of Nimrod AEW aircraft that were studied in early 1966, the four final answers being summarised in a brochure of August that year. Three had 180 degree dishes at nose and tail, and the fourth a very wide but shallow dish rotating inside a fixed dorsal radome. A crucial factor was that the radar had to work well over the open ocean, as well as over land.

The various radar options had by this time become the largest single research programme at the Royal Radar Establishment (RRE) at Great Malvern, Worcestershire. By the late-1960s the RRE had come down firmly in favour of an FMICW radar, with an inverted-Cassegrain dish at nose and tail. This had so many things to commend it, especially for oceanic operations, that in 1971 the special Comet 4, XW626, based at the Aeroplane & Armament Experimental Establishment at Boscombe Down, Wiltshire, was returned to

Hawker Siddeley's Chester factory, in order to have such an antenna mounted on the nose. The intention was that the production AEW platform should be based on either the Comet or a Nimrod. Seeing this, the Treasury was horrified at such an expensive solution, and immediately cut off all funding. The embryonic 180 degree radar was returned to Malvern, and the Comet was sent back to gather dust at Boscombe Down. Instead, the Treasury decreed that the future AEW aircraft should be based on the Andover, a turboprop aircraft even smaller than the Shackleton, with totally inadequate range, endurance and operating altitude, and unable to house the radar.

It took a further year for such a ludicrous notion to fade, but the possibility of actual progress at last emerged February 1972, when it was realised that the first Boeing AWACS (pronounced 'A-waks', and meaning airborne warning and control system) for the US Air Force was already being flight tested. Originally planned around four pairs of General Electric TF34 turbofans, this had finally emerged as the Boeing E-3 Sentry, based on a 707-320C airframe, carefully

XW626 making a slow fly-past with landing gear extended. (*Philip Jarrett*)

planned to make the best use of a pylon-mounted 30 ft (9.14 m) rotodome, rotating at 6 r.p.m. Much larger than the Nimrod, and with almost double the gross weight, it had the salutary effect of forcing the British Treasury to consider more sensible solutions to the Shackleton replacement problem. The obvious platform was the Nimrod. Trickle funding was released later in 1972, to permit a feasibility study to begin. The contractors were Hawker Siddeley's Avro Whitworth division, at Manchester, and the Marconi-Elliott company, at Rochester, Kent, and Boreham Wood, in Hertfordshire. Project definition of what had become designated as the Nimrod AEW.3 was carried out in 1973.

Having studied the problem so often, the two prime contractors knew from the start what they considered to be the best answer, but they wasted more time going through the motions of evaluation against three possible alternatives. The first option was, in effect, the E-2C Hawkeye, with the airframe changed to the Nimrod. The second option was an attempt to mount the Hawkeye's radar, which at that time was the General Electric APS-125, on a Nimrod housing British electronics. The third option matched the Randtron APN-171 antenna and radome with a British radar and avionics. The final option was an updated form of the brilliant 1966 proposal to fit all-British systems, and to continue to develop the radar with 180 degree antennas on the nose and tail. One of the few good choices was that in late-1974 this final option was selected. At last, the RRE and Marconi-Elliott were able to carry on from where they had been forced to leave off three years previously.

Even then, it was by no means plain sailing. Naturally, Boeing was determined to sell the E-3A Sentry to the European members of NATO and mounted a convincing campaign. In April 1974 a pre-production E-3A came to Europe to help clinch the deal, which to virtually all the European defence staffs was the obvious answer. Britain was strongly pressed to come on board with the E-3A, while Britain made no attempt to interest its NATO partners in the AEW Nimrod. In 1975 NATO opened formal negotiations for an international force equipped with the E-3A. The idea was that, with Britain participating, the force should be based at RAF Waddington, Lincolnshire. In December 1978 the European NATO countries signed for eighteen E-3A aircraft, and, as Britain was now absent, the operating base was changed to the former RAF station, now a Luftwaffe base, at Geilenkirchen, in West Germany.

Britain alone was determined to pursue a national solution, largely because of its unique need for an AEW aircraft 'to provide at long range, and at low or high altitude, detection, tracking and classification of aircraft, missiles and ships; interceptor control; direction of strike aircraft; air defence; air-traffic control; and search and rescue facilities'. Typically, it took several years for the Operating Specification of the planned Nimrod AEW.3 to be agreed, and it was not issued, as ASR. (Air Staff Requirement) 400, until mid-1976. The E-3A could not meet several of the British requirements, including the crucial one of finding small objects at sea, such as a submarine's periscope. Moreover, at the low operating height of 20,000 ft (6 km) the E-3A would fly at an angle of attack of about 4 degrees, making the whole area underneath blind out to 45 miles (72 km) ahead. At the normal patrol height of over 30,000 ft (9 km), the blind area is much greater.

By 1975, the forlorn Comet XW626 had, for the second time, been flown to Woodford, and the RRE and several contractors had virtually completed the basic design of the radar. It then took two further years to install the experimental forward-looking radar in the aircraft. At last, it was rolled out on 1 March 1977, and because at that time NATO had still not actually placed an order for the Boeing E-3A, the occasion was turned into a publicised ceremony, though it could hardly have been expected to be of any interest to the European NATO members. On 31 March 1977, the Minister of Defence, Fred Mulley, announced an order for eleven Nimrod AEW.3 aircraft, all of them to be rebuilds of existing Nimrod MR.2s. These were supposed to cost £300 million, but the amazing decision had been taken to award what had now become GEC Marconi *an open contract*, so the final price could be anything considered necessary. The trials Comet XW626 began flight testing on 28 June 1977.

Obviously, it was the start of a massive development programme, which was almost immediately thrown into confusion by the issue of ASR.400 Revision 1, with no instructions on which items were affected by the new standard, and which were not. Another factor which did not help was that, despite the shocking lesson of TSR.2, the overall management structure had if anything, got even worse. There is not sufficient room here to outline the convoluted family tree of project management for the aircraft, and the quite different, and even more convoluted, chain of command for the radar and other avionics. It was all in stark contrast to the USAF, which appoints a single outstanding officer, for an important programme a brigadier-general, who runs the whole show at a brisk pace, with tight control, until the system is in full service.

Comet XW626 is seen here with the unique Bedford-based Canberra WT333, known as the B(I)8/6, because it was a B(I). 8 which in 1976 was fitted with the nose of a B.6. It assisted in AEW.3 radar development, and is today preserved at Bruntingthorpe. *(Philip Jarrett)*

As explained in Chapter 6, the AEW programme was considered so important that the eleven Nimrods allocated for conversion were those with the lowest flight time. It is typical of British defence procurement that, in an environment of crippling financial stringency, the second batch of eight Nimrod MR.1s had been intended to equip a squadron based on Malta GC, but were actually ordered just as the United Kingdom was withdrawing from that island, making these aircraft redundant. Thus, the eleven aircraft selected were XV259, 261, 262 and 263; and XZ280, 281, 282, 283, 285, 286 and 287. The first development Nimrod AEW.3, XZ286, was rolled out at Woodford on 30 March 1980, and began flight testing on 16 July 1980. After a prolonged gap, the first production aircraft, XZ285, followed on 9 March 1982. By this time work appeared at last to be going well, and RAF Waddington was a hive of activity as it converted from the Vulcan to the AEW Nimrod.

The first AEW.3; essentially complete.

Conversion of an MR.2 to an AEW.3 obviously involved removing the deep weapons bay and its covering structure, making the basic fuselage broadly similar to that of a Comet. The other visible change was to add the radar antennas at nose and tail. The antennas themselves were identical, each being an inverted-Cassegrain reflector, of elliptical profile, measuring 96 in × 72 in (2,438 mm × 1,829 mm), with a hyperboloid sub-dish. The unwanted sidelobes were reduced to an all-time low level. Scanning was mechanical, with precise control to sweep the nose and tail antennas to and fro in perfect synchronisation, each 180 degree sweep being followed by a rapid return with power switched off. Extremely precise mountings enabled the antenna gimbals to rotate gently in pitch and roll, to keep the antennas sweeping accurately, irrespective of aircraft manoeuvres.

For aerodynamic reasons the nose radome was quite pointed, while that at the tail was rounded. The rear fuselage was swept slightly up to avoid scraping the tail radome on the runway during take-off, while another modification was

A civilian test crew at work in one of the AEW.3 development aircraft, looking forwards.
(Philip Jarrett)

XZ285 trailing wingtip vortices.

to increase the span of the horizontal tail, and add 3 ft (0.91 m) to the height of the vertical tail. Despite the radically changed appearance of the aircraft, these radomes had only a slight affect on flight performance. Unlike the E-3A radar, the scanners did not suffer from a cyclic error, and they also differed in having a perfect view, not obscured by the aircraft itself.

The radar used pulse-doppler processing, and operated in the dual frequency bands 2 to 4 GHz. One of the requirements, demanded from the outset, was that it should be able to detect and track 400 targets simultaneously. Of course, everything possible was done to resist hostile jamming, and though details were classified, it could be said that the anti-ECM facilities were 'highly sophisticated'. Naturally, the IFF interrogation was done using the same antennas, this equipment being the Cossor Guardsman 3500. The only serious problems with the AEW Nimrod were that air-cooling the powerful radar and other electronics was difficult to achieve, and using the fuel as a heat sink would have severely curtailed mission endurance, because much of the hot fuel would have had to remain unused. Providing adequate air cooling was obviously a soluble problem. In any case, modern computers do not have to generate awesome amounts of heat. Today you can have megabytes in your pocket.

Backing up the radar were the mission-system avionics (MSA). This was centred on the GEC.4080M computer, which linked all the inputs from the scanners with all the outputs and displays. The storage capacity of 1 MB, with 1.4 MB available from a data-bus, was even at the time a sick joke. Many of those working on the programme could see that this was not just inadequate, but inadequate by about two powers of ten. Multiplying the capacity would have been perfectly simple, but permission to do so kept being withheld. Other equipment included the Loral ARI-18240/1 ESM (electronic surveillance measures).

Equipment in the cabin was arranged in groups, with communications at the front, displays amidships and data processing at the rear, and little need be added to that clarified by the cutaway drawing (page 130–1). As originally planned, the six operator stations in the forward fuselage were all identical. Routine functions such as association of radar, IFF and EWSM (electronic-warfare support measures), track initiation, tracking and data storage, were carried out automatically, requiring no operator input. When necessary, the operator interfaced by a rolling ball, or functionally arranged keyboards.

What might be called domestic avionics were generally similar to those of the Nimrod MR.2. The Ferranti FIN.1012 INS (inertial navigation system) automatically provided stabilisation of the aircraft in pitch and roll, and compensated for antenna inaccuracies caused by flexing of the airframe. Communications included Simop (simultaneous operation) h.f., tactical u.h.f., pilots' u.h.f./v.h.f., l.f. receiver, Ratt (radio teletype), secure-voice communications and data links. The Spey Mk 250 engine was unchanged, and the existing 60-kVA alternators provided adequate electrical power. This remained marginally sufficient when, during development, it was decided to add the Loral 1017 Yellow Knife pods on the wingtips, ahead of the main Nimrod force. Another addition, standard from the outset, was the flight-refuelling probe. These additions are described in Chapter 7.

In true British fashion, the Nimrod AEW.3 was a gigantic problem which, though perfectly capable of solution, was attacked by inadequate teams with extremely poor communications, in an environment of impossible, yet costly, funding. The MSA worked well in the laboratory, but in flight it was very different, only three hours of full-system operation being achieved in the first eight sorties. There is little point in relating all the problems and shortcomings, except to comment that every one was capable of solution.

Altogether, the Nimrod AEW.3 was potentially an outstanding surveillance platform. Developed in a sensible environment, it could have become important equipment in several air forces, especially those tasked with surveillance over oceanic areas as well as over land. Unfortunately, it had the misfortune to be developed by a country with a long history of nonsensical procurement, in which amateurs take the key decisions, contractors start by quoting impossibly optimistic time-scales and costs, and customers appear not to live in the real world. In the case of the Nimrod AEW.3 this crazy situation was made much worse by the fact that the main contractor had an open-ended contract, and the customer air force, and to a considerable degree also the Government, had a deep ingrained belief in buying American. Altogether the combination was lethal.

There is nothing wrong in a defence contractor being hard-pressed by the customer to do more, and to do it faster. It is possible to cross a fine line to a point where it becomes obvious that the customer is introducing so many changes that proper management and timekeeping become impossible and eventual collapse is inevitable. The author felt frustrated by watching this happen in the case of the AEW Nimrod, and to watch electronics engineers being driven to utter despair.

One can sympathise with GEC Avionics publicity manager Peter Simmons, who wrote, on 22 September 1986:

> GEC Avionics has today confirmed the success of the recent flight trials, which have demonstrated major improvements to the airborne early warning system. Post-flight analysis has positively confirmed that the radar displays, now free from clutter, show the expected improvements in tracking performance over land and sea.

Three days later, his company's contract was cancelled, and the AEW competition was reopened. In an acrimonious environment, the Ministry went through the motions of evaluating the Nimrod against the E-3A Sentry, Hawkeye, Orion and a fascinating proposal by Airship Industries. The politically obvious choice, the Sentry, was announced in December 1986, causing a replacement panic at RAF Waddington.

Predictably, to ensure that nothing could ever be resurrected, it was ordered that the eleven Nimrod AEW.3 aircraft should be scrapped. One, XV263, was flown to RAF Finningley, near Doncaster, and used for trade training. Most of the others were flown to Abingdon, south of Oxford, where they were broken up. Two ended up in Scotland, being dismantled at Kinloss and nearby Elgin. Unlike TSR.2, nobody has tried to put any of the parts back together.

GEC Marconi tried to continue development of the fore-and-aft scanner system, because they had no doubt whatsoever that it was the best answer, especially when oceanic missions were important. They tried to market an improved version of the AEW.3 system, named *Argus* (the Greek god with 100 eyes), starting with India and China. These countries showed little interest. They knew that the nose/tail idea would not work. The British Ministry of Defence said so.

In November 2008 the Israelis released preliminary details of the CAEW (conformal AEW) aircraft, based on the Gulfstream G550. It has a 180 degree scanner on the nose, and another on the tail. This arrangement was adopted because it was the best answer.

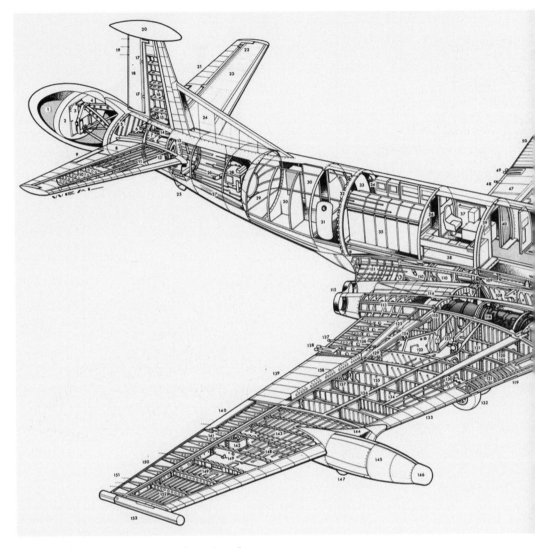

Nimrod AEW, cutaway drawing key

1 Tail radome
2 Aft radar aerial
3 Gyro stabiliser platforms
4 Tail radar mounting frame
5 Radome attachment
6 Elevator controls
7 Tailplane attachment frame
8 Starboard elevator
9 Elevator tab
10 Tailplane ribs
11 Tailplane forward spar
12 Tailplane spar/fuselage attachment

13 Fine attachment frame
14 Rudder control linkage
15 Fin attachment
16 Fin structure
17 Rudder hinges
18 Rudder
19 Static dischargers
20 Fin aerodynamic fairing
21 Port elevator
22 Elevator outer hinge
23 Port tailplane
24 Dorsal fin

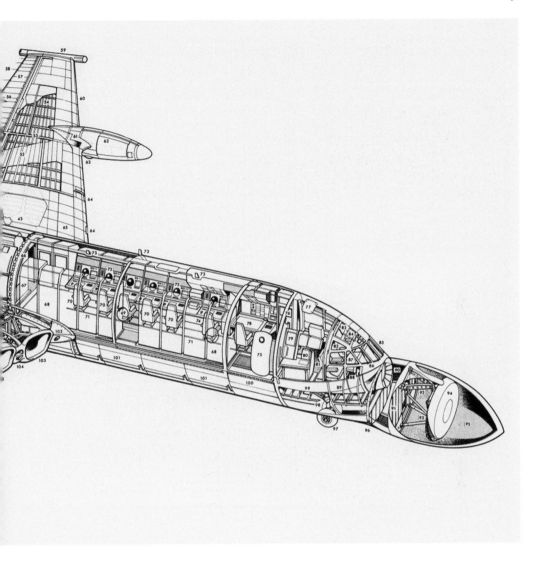

25 Tail bumper/fuselage vent
26 De-icing air supply duct
27 Rudder/elevator control rods
28 APU assembly
29 Rear pressure bulkhead
30 Equipment and spares stowage lockers
31 Emergency exit door
32 Fuselage frame
33 Aft entry door
34 Dorsal antenna
35 Radar equipment bays
36 Bulkhead
37 Crew rest area

38 Galley
39 Fuselage main frame
40 Bulkhead
41 Emergency escape window panel
42 ESM rack
43 Undercarriage bay upper surface panel
44 Machined inboard wing skin
45 Inboard airbrake (upper surfaces only)
46 Flap jack fairing
47 Flap inboard section
48 Fuel vent
49 Fuel dump pipes
50 Flap outer section

51 Outer airbrake (upper and lower surfaces)
52 Port wing integral fuel tanks
53 Skin butt-joint rib
54 Wing outer fuel tanks
55 Aileron tab
56 Aileron tab hinge fairing
57 Port aileron
58 Static dischargers
59 ESM port wingtip aerial
60 Wing leading edge
61 Fixed slot
62 External fuel tank
63 Wing tank bumper
64 Leading-edge flow spoilers
65 Integral fuel tank
66 Fuselage frame
67 Mission communications
68 Avionics modules
69 Window
70 Tactical crew seats: from front (right) to rear, communications control officer, ESM operator and three air direction officers
71 Seat rails
72 Tactical situation display consoles
73 Dorsal antennae
74 Tactical control officer
75 Crew entry door
76 Forward bulkhead
77 Emergency escape hatch
78 Navigator's station
79 Instrument consoles
80 Flight engineer's station
81 Co-pilot's seat
82 Cockpit roof structure
84 Pilot's seat
85 Windscreen panels
86 Windscreen wipers
87 Control console
88 Instrument panel
89 Support frames
90 Forward pressure bulkhead
91 Radome attachment
92 Nose radar mounting frame
93 Gyro stabiliser platforms
94 Nose radar aerial
95 Nose radome
96 Fuselage/radome fairing
97 Twin nosewheels
98 Nosewheel leg strut
99 Nosewheel well
100 Underfloor equipment bay
101 Fuel cells under cabin floor

102 Taxi light
103 Engine air intakes
104 Ram air to heat exchangers
105 Heat exchangers
106 Forward spar/fuselage attachment
107 Inboard engine bay (engine omitted)
108 Engine mounting frame
109 Rear spar/fuselage attachment
110 Life-raft stowage
111 Wingroot fillet structure
112 Exhaust pipes
113 Tailpipe frames
114 Thrust reverser (outboard engines only)
115 Rear spar frames
116 Rolls-Royce Spey 250 turbofan
117 Intake duct frames
118 Landing lamp
119 Leading-edge flow spoilers
120 Wing integral fuel tank
121 Forward spar
122 Main undercarriage pivot
123 Main undercarriage well
124 Rear spar
125 Inboard airbrake (upper surfaces only)
126 Flap structure
127 Fuel vent
128 Fuel dump pipes
129 Flap jack fairing
130 Wing skin joint strap
131 Leading-edge de-icing ducts
132 Four-wheel main undercarriage bogie
133 Wing leading-edge
134 Abbreviated spar
135 Integral fuel tanks
136 Centre spar
137 Airbrake mechanism
138 Outer airbrake (upper and lower surfaces)
139 Flap outer section
140 Aileron tab
141 Aileron tab hinge fairing
142 Aileron hinge control linkage
143 Wing stringers
144 Fixed slot
145 External fuel tank
146 Weather radar
147 Wing tank bumper
148 Outboard fuel tank bays
149 Fuel tank access panels
150 Starboard aileron
151 Static dischargers
152 Outboard wing structure
153 ESM starboard wingtip aerial

Chapter 10

The Nimrod MRA.4

The history related in this book includes so many cases of poor management, and politically contrived disaster, that it seems appropriate to conclude with one of the biggest examples of all of disastrous non-planning. With hindsight, it should have been quite straightforward, either to upgrade the existing Nimrods, or to design an all-new successor. What was actually done was to try to carry out an extremely challenging rebuild, in the worst way that could possibly have been devised.

This is particularly tragic, because the resulting Nimrod MRA.4 is – at the time of writing – the most capable and versatile multi-role platform in the world by a very clear margin. It has consistently had such a bad Press that it may surprise some readers to be told that each aircraft is almost a one-plane air force.

Looking back from 2009, it is hard to believe that, almost 20 years previously, in 1990, it was decided that the maritime-patrol Nimrod was reaching the end of its useful life, and that it was necessary to plan its replacement. At that time the emphasis was still centred on countering the menace of the Soviet Union's rapidly growing fleet of nuclear submarines, many of them armed with strategic missiles. Much time was spent detailing the complex portfolio of sensors and systems needed.

Thus, it was not until 1993 that ASR (Air Staff Requirement) 420 was at last issued. This document called for a Replacement Maritime Patrol Aircraft

(RMPA) for the RAF. The number required was between twelve and twenty-five, to be supplied by a single prime contractor. Moreover, in order to minimise risk (and hopefully cost, although this was not mentioned) the aircraft would be selected from an existing design. The requirements included a two-man cockpit, and an endurance exceeding 13 hours, with a time on station at a distance of 1,850 miles (2,980 km) of 8–10 hours, whilst carrying a formidable load of equipment and stores, which was listed in detail. Not least, the industrial teams were to offer 100 per cent offsets.

Bids were submitted in 1995. The candidates were: an updated Nimrod MR.2, called the BAe (British Aerospace) Nimrod 2000; the Lockheed Martin Orion 2000, based on the P-3C Update IV; the Lockheed Tactical Systems UK (formerly Loral) Valkyrie, a P-3A/B Orion rebuild; and the projected Dassault-Breguet *Atlantique* 3. In 1996 the *Atlantique* was withdrawn 'after the RAF's preference for a four-engined aircraft became clear'; how it took three years for this to 'become clear' (and for the second time) was not explained. In June 1996, McDonnell Douglas signed an agreement with BAe Systems to manufacture the Nimrod 2000 at St Louis, should it be selected by the US Navy to replace the P-3C. This proposition did get as far as a cursory evaluation.

At this time, BAe Systems was seriously short of work, and its bid was seen as a low-risk option, which would be able to use the existing Nimrod training and supporting infrastructure. Accordingly, the Ministry of Defence Equipment Approvals Committee recommended that the Nimrod 2000 should be selected. To the author, this choice appeared at the time to be obvious. Selection of the Nimrod 2000 was announced on 25 July 1996, when it was revealed that though these aircraft would be reconstructions of the existing Nimrod MR.2s, they would be '80 per cent new'.

Among other things, the wing centre section would be redesigned, for the fifth time, to accommodate the fifth change of engine, the Rolls-Royce (originally BMW Rolls-Royce) BR700. After this had been selected, BAe also studied another possibility, the General Electric CF34-8N. This would have required slightly less redesign of the wing, but other factors swung the balance back to the BR700. Other redesigned items would include the long-overdue updated cockpit, virtually all the accessory systems, and the complete avionics and mission systems. Later it was even decided that the main landing gears also had to be redesigned.

In late-December 1996 BAe was awarded a contract, MAR.21a/100, for '21 Nimrod 2000s, training systems and initial support'. The author was relieved to see that it was at least intended to be a fixed-price contract, but it was priced at 'up to £2.2 billion', or twenty-three times the price of the original thirty-eight Nimrod MR.1s. Work began at once converting three Nimrod MR.2s, which had been in storage at RAF Kinloss, to serve as a development batch (DB). The first delivery was due in 2001, followed by IOC (Initial Operational Capability) on delivery of the seventh aircraft in April 2003. The immediate work involved completely stripping the three DB aircraft of equipment, and dismantling the airframes. This enormous task was completed commendably quickly.

While the negotiations were in progress, BAe secured several important contracts, which over a matter of weeks, resulted in a sharply increased workload. In turn, this caused a critical shortage of engineers. In the United States, the simple answer would naturally have been to hire as many engineers as were necessary. In the UK, life is more difficult. After hectic meetings, it was decided to parcel out the Nimrod 2000 work between BAe (later BAE Systems) sites at Woodford, Chadderton, Brough and Filton, and to assign the final assembly of the bare unequipped aircraft to FRA-Serco at Hurn, near Bournemouth. In February 1997 an Antonov An-124, of Volga-Dniepr HeavyLift, delivered the stripped-down fuselages of the three DB aircraft from Kinloss to Hurn.

By this time, the MoD had realised that following the collapse of the Soviet Union, its pr-icipal successor Russia was no longer building nuclear submarines, and had tied up most of the existing ones. At the same time, it also belatedly recognised that the new Nimrod could become an exceptionally versatile multi-role platform. Accordingly, in early 1998 the Nimrod 2000 was redesignated as the Nimrod MRA.4, meaning Maritime Reconnaissance and Attack. Further new items of equipment were added, and because of the totality of the rebuild, they were assigned new serial numbers.

Any attempt to adhere to the original in-service date had by this time been abandoned. Uniquely, in January 1999 the complexity of the now more extensive systems-integration task resulted in Boeing being appointed integrator of what was now called the Tactical Command and Sensor System (TCSS), in some documents written Tactical Control and Sensor System. It was explained that this unprecedented decision was taken mainly because of the American company's experience on the P-3C Update IV and the 737 Surveiller. It was also considered to make adoption of the MRA.4 by the US Navy slightly less unlikely.

Almost from the outset, the decision to involve so many teams, at geographically distant sites, combined with abysmal communications and oversight, proved almost lethal to the entire programme. According to the then Chief of Defence Procurement, Sir Robert Walmsley: 'a weak management culture hugely underestimated the design challenge'. The one place where things worked on schedule was BMW Rolls-Royce (later Rolls-Royce Deutschland), at Dahlewitz, near Berlin. This new factory shipped all the BR710 engines on or ahead of time in 1999, but there were no airframes in which to install them.

In March 1999 it was announced that 'resource and technical difficulties … at BAe' had caused the first-flight date of the first aircraft to slip to late 2002, with an in-service date moved to early-2005. Again, the entire programme was torn up and redrafted. FRA-Serco, which had been frantically trying to get its factory ready for the assembly line, was abruptly eliminated. Instead, all manufacturing assembly was transferred to Woodford, whence the three DB fuselages were sent. Shortly afterwards it was decided that because of the strength of its technical manpower, the enormous task of fitting out the aircraft with mission equipment and carrying out flight testing, should be the responsibility of BAE Systems at Warton, near Preston, Lancashire. It was further agreed that each aircraft would be flown 'green' from Woodford to Warton.

Actual assembly of the first aircraft began on 6 September 2000, when the first wing centre section, a wholly new structure, and the heaviest single portion of the aircraft, was trucked from Chadderton to Woodford. However, by March 2002 the complexity of the task had resulted in the first of further revised schedules, which among other things cut the programme to only eighteen aircraft. Indeed, on 19 February 2003, the MoD and BAE Systems announced that, as a 'risk-reduction exercise', all work on aircraft beyond the DB would be halted.

By far the largest structural change was the new wing. Originally, it had been hoped to retain the existing outer panels, but despite the low flight time on the three DB wings, the RAF seemed to be so flush with excess money that it requested that the MRA.4 wing should be new from tip to tip. The first complete MRA.4 wing was scheduled to be mated with a spare Nimrod fuselage, to begin a 1,000-hour test in early 2004. By this time there were repeated rumours that the entire programme would be abandoned, but the Defence Review of July 2004 announced that it would continue, but was again being reduced, this time to a mere twelve, inclusive of the three DB aircraft.

Following assessment of new delivery dates and prices, a replacement contract was signed on 18 July 2006. By now, the total programme cost was estimated at £3.8 billion. In other words, the cost per aircraft had risen to £316.7 million, or over 125 times the cost of each Nimrod MR.1. This is surely some kind of disgraceful world record.

By this time, July 2006, the three DB aircraft were almost complete externally, though the giant task of fitting them out remained. Called PA (Prototype Aircraft), the three aircraft are:

PA-01, ZJ516 (ex-XV234): finished in Hemp, first test with full electrical power 19 December 2001, taxi testing from 12 June 2004, first flight (chief test pilot, John Turner) 26 August 2004, transit Woodford-Warton; assigned to aerodynamics, envelope clearance and expansion, and engines.

PA-02, ZJ518 (ex-XV247): finished in grey, first flight 15 December 2004, transit Woodford-Warton; assigned complete mission system, including weapon carriage and release.

PA-03, ZJ517 (ex-XV242): finished in grey, first flight 29 August 2005, transit Woodford-Warton; production standard, but with added instrumentation.

The progress of the programme, and the outline of difficulties and prospects, will be resumed after describing the aircraft as it was in mid-2008. As related at the end of Chapter 6, though the author finds it utterly beyond belief, it has been reported that a major reason for the fact that the programme has moved at such a slow pace is because the original Nimrod airframes were built most inaccurately, and that fuselage dimensions between one aircraft and the next might differ 'by as much as four inches' (over 10 cm). When one considers that the forty-nine aircraft were all constructed in precise jigging, and delivered at a high rate, there is no way such an error could have been introduced. One is left wondering whether the accurately built aircraft could each have had its fuselage over-stressed beyond the elastic limit in regular operational service. Again, this could not happen without the imposition of almost impossible stresses, which would have been reported and logged, making the aircraft immediately unserviceable.

As noted previously, whereas the upgrade from the Nimrod MR.1 to MR.2 standard hardly affected the airframe, that of the MRA.4 is loosely described as '80 percent new'. One of the few parts of the MRA.4 that is not newly built is the shell of the fuselage, and even this may have been a mistake. The fuselage has a new pressure-bearing floor from Frame 1 (nose) to Frame 54 (rear pressure bulkhead), and the retained structure incorporates replacement bulkheads, and is given new protective treatment. The front and lower fuselage structure was designed by BAe at Farnborough, the centre fuselage was designed at Prestwick, and the rear fuselage was (and still is) designed in France by Dassault, using CAD/CAM computerised calculations. The entire fuselages were then constructed at Brough, in East Yorkshire. Several frames in the forward fuselage carry a scabbed-on RAT (ram-air turbine) on the left side, and the right-hand door in the aft fuselage incorporates a deployable air dam, to assist in-flight emergency egress.

The new wing centre section, made at the former Avro factory at Chadderton, between Manchester and Oldham, has integral machined skins, and forms No.1 fuel tank. The new outer wings were designed at Filton, Bristol, and made at Prestwick, in Ayrshire. Curiously, except for the dorsal fin, the tail is described as being one of the few parts retained from the Nimrod MR.2, yet new 'tailplanes, elevators, and rudder, are designed at Prestwick and Farnborough, and built at Prestwick by FR Aviation' (FRA-Serco). The auxiliary fins, above and below the tailplanes, are of a new swept-back parallel-chord design, and made of composite material, while a visible change to the large dorsal fin is that it incorporates a ram-air intake at the root. The ventral fin is now protected by a tail bumper.

The BR700-710-48M two-shaft turbofan engines have the RAF designation BR700 Mk 101. They were designed and manufactured by Rolls-Royce Deutschland (RRD), at Dahlewitz. In 1996 this engine had a take-off rating of 14,900 lb (6,759 kg), but predictable aircraft weight growth required this to be increased to a fleet-average rating of 15,577 lb (7,066 kg). Geometrically, the big change is that, while the Spey had a low-pressure compressor, only slightly larger than the high-pressure spool immediately behind, the BR700 has a large single-stage fan on the front, which generates most of the thrust, and increases the bypass ratio to 5.2. Thus, the BR700 is much larger in diameter than the Spey, at 52 in (1,311 mm), and at 3,600 lb (1,633 kg) it is also heavier. Specific fuel consumption is considerably better, but directly comparable figures, either for take-off or cruise, have not been published.

There was no difficulty in accommodating the engine's length of 134 in (3,409 mm), but the diameter of 52 in resulted in very large inlets, and significant bulges in the wing, especially on the underside. As the aircraft required a new wing anyway, BAe looked carefully at the option of hanging the engines on under-wing pylons, but the tailplane could not handle the pitching moment from the lower thrust lines. Another arrangement considered was reminiscent of 1945 D.H.106 studies, with paired under-wing engines resembling Concorde. Instantly called 'the Conrod', this arrangement would have allowed a fully dressed engine to be removed straight downwards, but again, it was found to pose major problems.

Accordingly, the old wing-root installation was upgraded yet again. The all-new structure is stressed to the much greater gross weight, and the inboard wing is also increased in span by an impressive 6 ft (1.83 m) on each side. The inlet duct is squeezed above and below by the T-section booms of the main spar. These members are stiffened above and below each duct by curved bridge sections, which follow the periphery of the skin. Immediately behind the spar are removable inlet-duct adapter shells. The large engine-access doors are of thick sandwich construction, to retain maximum rigidity. The outer engines are significantly further aft than the inners, reflecting the 20 degree sweep of the spar. At the rear, the engine fan duct is connected by adapter shells to the shortest possible jetpipe, terminating just behind the trailing edge. Thanks to the relatively cool fan air, there is no need to angle the jetpipes outwards. Each engine is removed upwards, and its jetpipe to the rear. As take-off noise is reduced by over 90 per cent, compared with the Spey, there is no need for noise suppressors, but astonishingly there are no reversers. This is because the brakes are extremely powerful, as commented on later, and relying on them alone saves considerable weight. There are no inboard flaps.

The Dash-48M engine is almost identical to the Dash-48C series, which have logged many thousands of hours in the GV and Global Express business jets. It has the same Fadec (full-authority digital engine control), occupying a large box on top, but with usage and health-monitoring systems augmented by life-counting algorithms based on the system fitted to the EJ200 engine of the Eurofighter Typhoon. It retains the civil engine's pneumatic starting, including cross-bleed from a running engine, and has similar accessories, apart from an up-rated drive to a 40-kVA alternator. Nothing has been done which would invalidate civil clearances, although everything is marinised, as on earlier Nimrods.

Vibro-Meter UK supply a 35-item system which integrates the engines' high-energy ignition system with sensors for shaft speeds, air, oil and fuel temperatures, oil and fuel pressures, and oil-debris monitoring. In 1997 RRD signed a contract to deliver eighty-seven Nimrod engines, and no information has been found on how this has been cut, if at all. In RAF service, the engines will be serviced by Rolls-Royce plc at East Kilbride, near Glasgow.

With a totally new wing, the fuel system is completely redesigned. There are now thirteen tanks, eight more than in early Comets, linked into an automated system. Wing tanks 2, 3 and 4 can be gravity-filled through over-wing caps, but normally the entire system is pressure-fuelled, either by a single under-wing socket, or by the flight-refuelling probe. The system can be filled from empty in 30 minutes, even though its capacity is increased to 13,540 gallons (16,263 US gallons, 61,561 litres, 108,981 lb, 49,434 kg). With no flight engineer in the crew, great care has been taken in designing the largely automated fuel-system management, by USMS computers. In view of the serious difficulties being encountered with the Nimrod MR.2, particular attention has been paid to making the MRA.4 fuel system as foolproof and fireproof as possible.

The automatic flight-control system (AFCS) is upgraded to provide additional operating modes, and is linked to a GPWS (ground-proximity warning system). A novel feature is that, should any surface power unit jam (lock-up solid), that power unit can be taken out of circuit, and the aircraft flown without control degradation on whichever aileron or elevator remains operable. With an aircraft as complex as the MRA.4, a simplified description has to skate over many topics, and it is impossible here to reproduce the fascinating 2007 Roy Chadwick Lecture of the Royal Aeronautical Society, which dealt solely with the MRA.4 pitch-control (elevator) system. Suffice to say, it is light-years beyond that of the Comet and Nimrod MR.2 – but it still gave trouble in flight testing.

The electrical system is an updated form of that in the MR.2, with each busbar connected to its own 40-kVA integrated-drive generator. The specially designed APU (auxiliary power unit) is a Honeywell product, designated as the 300–200(N), located in a fireproof box in the right wing root. It provides up to

90 kVA of electrical power, plus bleed air for engine starting, on the ground only. A ram-air turbine (RAT) is scabbed into the left side of the fuselage ahead of the left wing. In the event of total loss of electrical power, the RAT drives an alternator supplying current to the Yellow System (see Chapter 2) hydraulic pump.

The extensive air-conditioning system incorporates four conditioning packs, two of them being in the rear fuselage, fed from the ram-air inlet at the base of the fin. The oxygen system is fed from an Obogs (on-board oxygen-generating system), with a back-up pressure cylinder, and portable sets for anyone moving about the cabin. The hydraulics are not greatly changed, but there is a very complete utilities-systems management system.

Though it does not look very different, the main landing gear, made by Messier-Dowty, is completely redesigned. The main structure is now in high-strength steel, matched to the considerably increased gross weight, with multi-plate 'heat-pack' carbon brakes, and tyres unchanged in size but inflated to a higher level called PR24. The nose landing gear is also new, with PR14 tyres and 'steer-by-wire'.

The entire under-floor structure has been redesigned, but it remains unpressurised. At the nose is the radar, which had to be new, to cater for the much wider variety of missions. Initially BAe selected the Israeli Elta EL.2020. Reportedly on political grounds, this was replaced by a Thales Sensors (Racal) radar called Searchwater 2000MR. This is integrated into the Boeing-managed TCSS, and as in previous Nimrods, the display is in the cockpit, enabling the radar operator to be dispensed with. Target classification is carried out using range profiling and synthetic image-processing. Operating modes include maritime reconnaissance, air-to-air, weather, SAR, and SAR using spotlight or ISAR (inverse synthetic-aperture radar), I-band transponder, and D-band IFF interrogator.

To the rear of the radar is the nose gear, and behind that a retractable EOSDS turret, described later. This is followed by the capacious weapons bay, covered as before by front and rear pairs of doors. At the tail is a compartment from which a towed radar decoy can be unreeled. Modern equipment and displays have enabled the normal mission crew to be reduced to seven: Tacco 1 and 2, radar, communications, ESM and Acoustics 1 and 2. All seating is crashworthy, cleared to 16 g, supplied by Martin-Baker. Domestic provisions include a refrigerator and oven, water boiler, sink and potable-water treatment unit.

The cockpit is generally unchanged, retaining a jump seat for a third person, but the instrument panels are totally different. Instrumentation is dominated by seven Thales displays, basically the same 8 in × 8 in (20 cm × 20 cm) multifunction units as are fitted to the Airbus A330 and 340. These provide everything the pilots wish to know, and as far as possible eliminate anything that is not of current interest. As a back-up, there are also eleven traditional dial instruments, a surprisingly large number.

The MRA.4 systems-integration possibly exceeds in magnitude anything required in any previous aircraft. Developing it involved meeting over 4,000 customer (MoD) requirements. The avionics systems alone require more than 90 sensors and antennas, over 1,500 major bought-out items, and more than 1,000 line-replaceable units. The on-board computers incorporate over 6 million lines of software code. Despite this complexity, the MRA.4 has been designed to require 'less than half the maintenance of any comparable aircraft'. An innovative feature is Airbus-style instant readout of any problem. Maintenance targets include an A-check once a year, and a C-check once every six years. For each sortie, the planning data from Permanent Joint Headquarters at Northwood, Middlesex, are unloaded into the Mission Support System, and brought on board as a compact cartridge, replacing the reams of paper used on each Nimrod MR.2 mission.

Navigation is controlled by the Flight Management System (FMS), interfacing with the FDDS (flight-deck display system), AFCS (automatic flight-control system), and the aircraft sensor systems, such as temperature, and pitot and static pressure. The FMS has two MCDUs (multifunctional control and display units), which control the tuning of the radio-navigational systems. Equipment includes dual Litton LN-1006 laser INS with embedded GPS, BAE Systems ILS/VOR/MLS and DME, Rockwell Collins ADF, Tacan and TCAS II (traffic-alert and collision-avoidance system), Thales radar altimeters, and a triple air-data system.

Communications, assigned to Telephonics, required no fewer than five v.h.f./u.h.f. radios, incorporating the Have Quick secure-speech facility. There are two other u.h.f. radios, and a Thales IFF Mode S transponder. All these items, and the fibre-optics intercom system, are managed by the radio communications system (RCS), which integrates navigation and communications, internal voice communication and warning tones. Ultra Electronics provides Link-11 communications, Rockwell Collins Link-16 (JTIDS, joint tactical information distribution system), MBDA the s.h.f. (super-high-frequency) satcom link, Raytheon the u.h.f. satcom link, and a teletype modem. Clearly, unlike previous versions, the MRA.4 has outstanding capability as a battlefield command and control platform.

The most complex system of all, managed by Boeing, is the TCS, originally the Tactical Command System, but later, with the proliferation of missions, restyled the Tactical Command and Sensor System. An indication of the magnitude of the development task is afforded by the fact that creating it involved engineers from Seattle, Huntsville, Houston, Philadelphia and St Louis, as well as 120 from the UK, and that the initial contract was priced at $639 million. The system links all mission systems and sensors, conforming throughout to the standard MIL-STD-1760 database for digital systems. It enables the MRA.4's human crew to manage the tactical situation, flight control and navigation, mission sensors, stores, communications and defensive-aids subsystems. The system is managed from seven identical Boeing-supplied consoles. Each subsystem incorporates BIT (built-in test) functions. Showing strategic vision all too rare in British defence procurement, there is provision for three additional workstations, for further-developed, new or special-fit equipment that might be invented in the future.

One of the new items is the Night Hunter EOSDS, the electro-optical surveillance and detection system, supplied by Northrop Grumman. This is housed in a turret, which can be extended down from a compartment behind the nose landing gear. It was mainly to counter the predicted yaw, caused by extension of this turret, that the auxiliary fins were added to the tailplane. The turret provides 360 degree surveillance of the entire region below the aircraft, including tracking through nadir (vertically downwards) with two TV cameras and two IR (infra-red) cameras. Images from any two wavelengths can be fused into a single false-colour picture, for display on a monitor. The EOSDS is controlled from the No.2 console.

Ultra Electronics supply the Cambs VI command active-search sonobuoy system, with five antennas linking the sonobuoy(s) with the onboard receiver subsystem, processor subsystems and acoustics recorder. The antennas comprise a primary antenna, which receives the buoy's RF (radio-frequency) data, and a four-blade array whose main function is indicating the buoy's exact position.

PA-01/ZZ516 on take-off on 22 September 2005. (*Neville Beckett*)

Grey-painted PA-02/ZZ518 at Warton. (*Neville Beckett*)

PA-02/ZZ518 is seen here after more than four years of flight-testing, with a camera on the underwing stores pylon, and a static line from the right wingtip.

An extensive receiver subsystem provides many functions, including routing of signals to receivers, preservation of phase-integrity from the array, and frequency translation of SAR (search and rescue) signals. Computing Devices Canada/ Ultra Electronics supply the UYS-503/AQS-970 APSS (acoustics processor subsystem). This comprises a control unit, and four automatic data-processors. All data are recorded.

Racks are provided in the rear of the cabin for 180 sonobuoys, but if necessary 360 can be carried. These are dispensed through four Normalair-Garrett rotary launchers, each holding ten Size-A buoys. As in the Nimrod MR.2, there is a single launcher for use when the interior is pressurised.

The MAD in the tailboom remains the Canadian Aviation Electronics ASQ-504(V), integrated into the digital AQS-970 processor. The dedicated ESM (electronic surveillance measures) sensor is the Elta EL/L-8300UK, served by a rotating antenna beneath the fuselage, able to pan through ±35 degrees in the vertical plane. This is used mainly for detecting RF (primarily radar) for classification, providing instant warning of illumination by any hostile emitter.

Though derived from that in the Nimrod MR.2, the defensive-aids subsystem (DASS) is considerably updated and augmented, Lockheed Martin being the principal integrator. This company itself supplies the ALR-56M(V) C/D-band and E/K-band RWR (radar warning receivers); in partnership with Thales, the twelve Vicon 78 payload dispensers (eight chaff, four flare); in conjunction with Sanders, the AAR-57 MAW (missile-approach warner); and, in partnership with Raytheon, the ALE-500(V) active towed radar jammer, which is streamed from the tail end of the fuselage near the junction with the MAD. Interoperability of radiators and sensors is ensured by the Lockheed Martin/ Lambda MX-18296/A system manager.

Compared with the Nimrod MR.2, the MRA.4 carries a considerably wider range of weapons, for an unprecedented variety of missions. It also features a new armament control system, provided by Smiths, derived from that developed for the Boeing F/A-18 Hornet. It comprises the stores-management system, and the tactical command and sensor system, which manages the selection of stores, carriage, release and jettison, together with selection and release of sonobuoys. Whereas the MR.2 has two hardpoints to which under-wing stores pylons could be attached, but were seldom used, the MRA.4 has four multipurpose pylons as standard. Though similar in size to that of the MR.2, the weapon bay has been redesigned to accept any existing or future weapon procured to the MIL-STD-1760 Class II standard. Internal loads could include six Harpoon missiles, or SLAM-ER (four external), ten mines (four external), nine Sting Ray torpedoes (none external), five packs of three dinghies or rescue containers, twelve survival containers, or a single pod of thirty-six light series stores. Should the MRA.4 become operational, it will almost certainly be cleared to launch the Storm Shadow cruise missile. Each weapon load can be accompanied by an external load of four AGM-65 Maverick or other ASMs (air-to-surface missiles), or four Alarm, Asraam or Sidewinder AAMs (air-to-air missiles).

One unexpected problem, which surfaced before the first flight, was that the brakes needed careful adjustment. At maximum weight they were powerful enough to overstress the main gears, so the software was rewritten to prevent this. Initially the brakes also had a tendency to grab unexpectedly, and the cure here was to change the geometry of the cockpit pedals. A totally different problem was that the flight controls were noticeably heavier than those of the MR.2, needing greater pilot strength, especially in roll. This also was eventually ironed out. A more intractable problem was a tendency to porpoise (pitch/roll) under certain conditions, making the ride eventually seem unpleasant. Such characteristics can be tedious to rectify. As noted previously, some observers blamed this problem on the decision to retain the existing tailplane size and moment arm. As an immediate fix an SAS (stability-augmentation system) was quickly devised by BAE Systems Electronics and Integrated Solutions at Rochester, Kent.

As noted previously, the first MRA.4 to fly was PA-01, serial ZJ516, which in a very incomplete state was delivered from Woodford to Warton on 26 August 2004. The next to fly, on 15 December 2004, was PA-02, ZJ518. In early 2005 this aircraft was being lowered by crane into a harness for resonance testing. Unexpectedly, the rear bogie wheels hit the floor first, almost rolling the aircraft out of its cradle. Even though this did not happen, inspecting for possible damage cost several months.

At last, in early August 2005, PA-02 was declared airworthy again, and a joint BAE/RAF crew carried out a very successful series of trials from Sigonella, Sicily, in ambient temperatures up to 40° C (104° F). Sqn. Ldr. Drew Steel, leader of the RAF test team, commented at this time on the excellent stall-testing, during which PA-02 had flown at the extraordinary AOA (angle of attack) of 26 degrees. In September 2005 PA-02 arrived at Eglin AFB, Florida, for seven weeks of testing in temperatures ranging from -40°C/F up to 44°C (110°F), with a humidity of 100 per cent. In late-November 2005 the structural-test wing, called PA-56 and originally intended for aircraft PA-04, was delivered to Brough and mated with the fuselage, which came from an AEW.3, XV263.

In May 2007 PA-03 spent two days at Kinloss, from where it flew a test mission. On 14 July 2007 PA-02 appeared at the RAF Tattoo, and on the 19th of that month released a Sting Ray torpedo over the Aberporth range. On 18 February 2008 PA-01, with the Stability Augmentation System installed, visited Nashville International Airport in Tennessee for prolonged icing trials, using special instrumentation. PA-02 spent spring 2008 undertaking EMH (electro-magnetic hazard) tests, including 50,000-Volt simulated lightning strikes.

By late-February 2008 the three DB aircraft had passed the 1,000-hour mark, and by mid-2008 the D&D (design and development) phase was almost complete. Provided the Treasury do not succeed in forcing through supposed cheaper alternatives, the remaining nine aircraft were then making fair progress. PA-04, ZJ514 (ex-XV251) was 83 per cent complete, and externally appeared virtually finished, PA-05, ZJ515 (ex-XV251) was 62 per cent complete, PA-06, ZJ519 (ex-XZ284) was mated with its wing and 54 per cent complete, and PA-07,

ZJ520 (ex-XV233), PA-08, ZJ521 (ex-XV227), PA-09, ZJ522 (ex-XV245), PA-10, ZJ523 (ex-XV228), PA-11, ZJ524 (ex-XV243) and PA-12, ZJ525 (ex-XV246) were all stripped at Woodford, awaiting transfer to the production line. In 2008 PA-01 and PA-02 carried out airfield performance trials on the 5-km (16,400-ft) runway at Istres, near Marseilles. Testing included:

- Long taxi runs of up to 6.8 miles (11 km), with brakeless decelerations.
- Accelerate-stop tests at different weights, and to different speeds, including using maximum brake power to stop from 125 kt at MTOW.
- Refining the take-off technique and measuring speeds and distances.
- Determining the minimum speed at which take-off can be safely continued following various engine failures, including measuring the pilot's ability to maintain directional control.
- Assessing how the aircraft performs with trim not correctly set for take-off.

Afterwards, Steve Timms, the MRA.4 programme Managing Director, said:

> The trials have been extremely successful, with excellent aircraft reliability throughout. The fact that we were able to operate so successfully overseas shows the growing maturity of the MRA.4 platform. Over one two-week period PA-01 achieved 25 flights … We've now completed around 400 flights, in over 1,300 hours. Qualification of the aircraft's systems is almost complete, and we are making good progress towards the planned in-service date.

A major milestone towards that goal was the news on 27 November 2008 that the first production aircraft, PA-04, had been 'powered up' for the first time. As full electrical power coursed through the aircraft, test engineers worked through long investigatory procedures 'without a hitch'. Structurally 93 per cent complete, the aircraft can now be equipped with its mission systems and sensors, ready for further testing. Following initial testing on the runway at Woodford, PA-04, ZJ514, flew to Norwich airport on 10 September 2009 where it is being painted by Air Livery plc.

After taking far too long, and costing far too much, the programme should, as noted above, adhere to the scheduled ISD (in-service date) of December 2010.

There should then be five aircraft (four serviceable), six combat-ready crews, fully adequate engineering staff, and spares, and supporting infrastructure for on-going operations. The 12th MRA.4 should be complete 'by 2012', where-upon Woodford is expected to close.

This book has told a story unique in its mix of triumph and disaster. The first disasters were unwittingly caused by the people who designed and made the air-craft. All the subsequent ones have been the result of politicians and civil servants, who do not understand the problems, do not foresee the future, and cannot fore-tell the long-term results of trying to save money. Except for simple light-planes, the Nimrod MRA.4 is the last British aeroplane. In the author's opinion, the old cry 'British is Best' could eventually have applied to the Nimrod AEW.3, and is certainly true right now for the MRA.4. Trouble is, the grass is always greener.

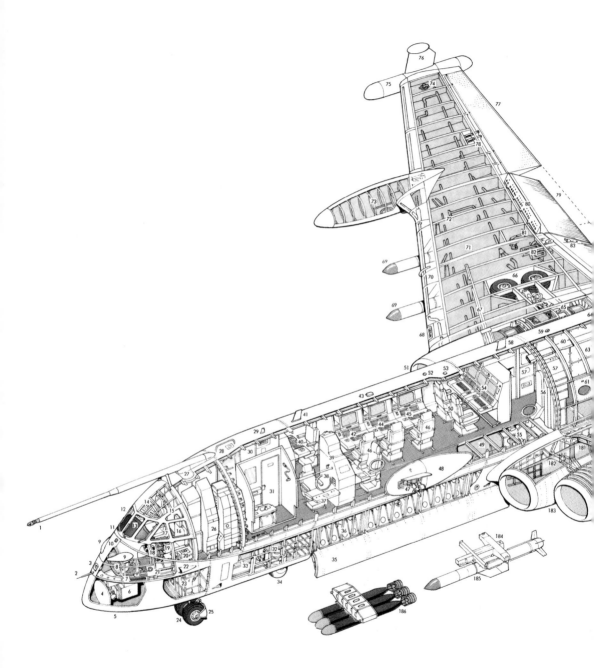

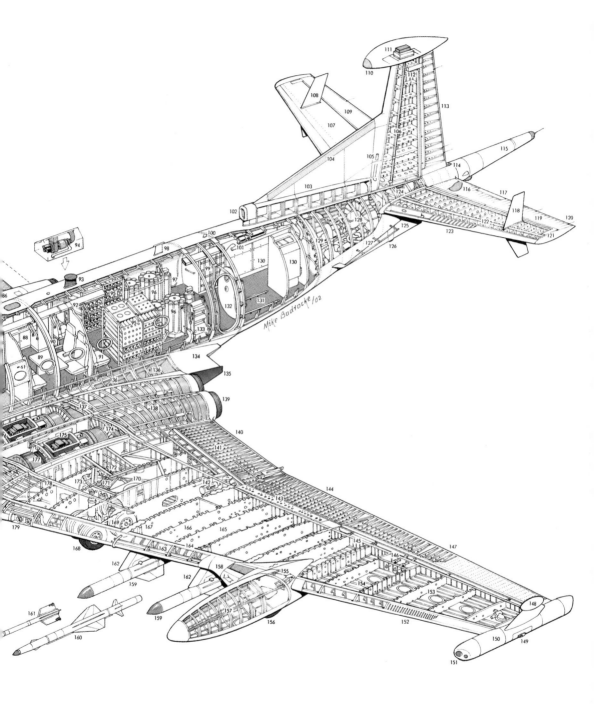

Mike Badrocke/02

British Aerospace Nimrod MRA.4, cutaway drawing key

1 Flight refuelling probe
2 Stand-by pitot head
3 Taxying light
4 Search radar scanner
5 Nose compartment radome
6 Scanner mounting
7 ILS antenna
8 Front pressure bulkhead
9 Forward ESM antenna fairings, port & starboard
10 MLS antenna
11 Windscreen wipers
12 Electrically heated windscreen panels
13 Instrument panel shroud
14 Overhead switch panel
15 Eyebrow window
16 Pilot's seat, two-pilot flight deck
17 Direct vision window panel
18 Instrument panel with Multi-function EFIS displays
19 Control column yoke
20 Side console panel with nosewheel steering tiller
21 Pitot head
22 Avionics cooling ram air intake
23 Nose undercarriage leg housing
24 Twin nosewheels, aft retracting
25 Fixed mudguards
26 Forward fuselage electrics and avionics racks
27 Cockpit roof hatch, inoperative with refuelling boom fitted
28 Starboard side forward entry door
29 TCAS antenna
30 Starboard side avionics racks
31 Crew toilet compartment
32 Ventral equipment bay
33 Nose undercarriage wheel bay
34 Electro-optical scanner turret
35 Forward weapons bay doors
36 Weapons bay 'pannier' sidewall structure
37 Port beam lookout station
38 Bulged observation window
39 Radar workstation
40 ESM workstation
41 Combined VHF/UHF/IFF antenna
42 Communications workstation
43 MLS antenna
44 TACCO 1 workstation
45 TACCO 2 workstation
46 Fully adjustable individual crew seats on sliding rail mounts

47 Emergency Ram-Air Turbine (RAT), extended
48 RAT housing, external to fuselage pressure shell
49 Underfloor fuel cells, fore and aft
50 Acoustic operators seats (2)
51 Starboard outer engine air intake
52 GPS 1 antenna
53 MW sensor
54 Acoustic workstation
55 Underfloor hydraulics equipment bay
56 Front spar mounting fuselage main bulkhead
57 Electrical equipment racks, port and starboard
58 VHF/UHF antenna
59 Strobe light
60 Forward cabin conditioned air ducting
61 Escape hatches, port and starboard
62 Wing centre-section with integral fuel tank
63 Fuselage centre avionics equipment racks
64 GPS 2 antenna
65 Starboard outer engine bay
66 Starboard main undercarriage, stowed position
67 Semi-span stub main spar
68 Leading edge landing lights
69 Starboard underwing missile carriage
70 Leading edge de-icing air ducting
71 Starboard wing integral fuel tankage
72 Fuel transfer and vent piping
73 Fixed external fuel tank
74 Vent surge tank
75 Wing tip ESM equipment pod
76 Winglet mounted ESM antenna
77 Starboard aileron
78 Aileron tandem hydraulic actuators
79 Outboard plain flap segment, down position
80 Starboard airbrake panel (open), upper and lower surfaces
81 Fuel collector tank with boost pumps
82 Starboard hydraulic flap actuator
83 Flap interconnecting link
84 Fuel vent
85 Inboard flap segment, down position
86 Starboard engine exhaust fairing
87 ADF antenna
88 Galley
89 Dinette
90 Rear spar mounting fuselage main frame
91 Passenger seats (2)

92 Rear cabin conditioned air distribution duct
93 JTIDS antenna
94 Auxiliary Power Unit (APU) mounted in starboard wing root fairing
95 Sonobuoy racks, port and starboard
96 Rotary sonobuoy launchers (4)
97 Pressurised single sonobuoy launchers (2)
98 VHF/UHF antenna
99 Crew wardrobe
100 TACAN antenna
101 Conditioned air mixing ducts
102 Conditioning system ram-air intake
103 Extended fin root fairing
104 Flush HF antennas
105 Fin de-icing air duct
106 Fin rib structure
107 Starboard tailplane
108 Auxiliary fins above and below
109 Starboard elevator
110 Fin tip 'canoe' antenna fairing
111 SATCOM antenna
112 Rudder mass balance
113 Rudder rib structure
114 Tail navigation light
115 Extended tailcone
116 Aft ESM antennae
117 Elevator trim tab
118 Port auxiliary fins
119 Port elevator
120 Static dischargers
121 Elevator mass balance
122 Tailplane rib structure
123 Tailplane leading thermal edge de-icing
124 Fin and tailplane mounting bulkhead
125 Ventral fin
126 Tail bumper
127 HF antenna rail
128 Dual air conditioning packs
129 Fuselage rear pressure bulkhead
130 Rear fuselage avionics equipment racks, port and starboard
131 Tie-down rails, crew baggage storage
132 In opening rear entry door
133 Airstairs stowed position
134 Wing root trailing edge fairing
135 Exhaust shroud
136 Wing root fuel tank bays
137 Rear spar exhaust duct forged and machined bulkhead
138 Jet pipes
139 Port engine exhausts
140 Port inboard plain flap segment
141 Flap rib structure
142 Flap hydraulic actuator
143 Port airbrake panel, upper and lower surfaces
144 Outer plain flap segment
145 Rear spar
146 Aileron dual hydraulic actuators
147 Port aileron rib structure
148 Port winglet mounted ESM antenna
149 Port navigation light
150 Wingtip ESM pod
151 High and low band ESM antennas, fore and aft
152 Leading edge thermal de-icing ducting
153 Outer wing panel rib structure
154 Wing bottom skin/stringer panel with access manholes
155 External fuel tank mounting
156 Tank protective bumper
157 Port external fuel tank
158 Slotted tank fairing
159 AGM-84 Harpoon air-to surface anti-shipping missile
160 ALARM anti-radiation missile, capacity for future integration
161 AIM-9L Sidewinder 'self-protection' air-to-air missile potential for future integration on lateral stub pylons
162 Port wing stores pylons
163 Inboard leading edge de-icing air duct
164 Front spar
165 Port wing integral fuel tank
166 Machined wing ribs
167 Outer wing panel joint rib
168 Port main undercarriage four-wheel bogie
169 Mainwheels with multi-plate carbon brakes
170 Wheel bay with pre-closing mainwheel door
171 Breaker strut and retraction linkage
172 Hydraulic retraction jack
173 Mainwheel leg pivot mounting
174 Engine bay firewalls
175 Full Authority Digital Engine Control unit (FADEC)
176 Main engine mounting beams
177 BMW Rolls-Royce BR710 turbofan engine
178 Port semi-span main spar
179 Port landing lights
180 Intake duct frame structure
181 Forged and machined intake duct bulkhead
182 Main spar-to-centre-section joint
183 Port engine air intakes
184 Weapons bay missile carrier/launcher
185 AGM-84 Harpoon, 2-in internal weapons bays
186 Stingray torpedoes

	Comet 1	Comet C.2	Comet 3	Comet 4	Comet 4B	Comet 4C
Engines (4)	D.H. Ghost 50	R-R Avon Mk 117	R-R Avon Mk 523	R-R Avon Mk 524	R-R Avon Mk 525B	R-R Avon 525C
Take-off thrust	5,000 lb (2,268 kg)	7,300 lb (3,311 kg)	10,000 lb (4,536 kg)	10,500 lb (4,763 kg)	10,500 lb (4,763 kg)	10,500 lb (4,763 kg)
Span	114 ft 10 in (35 m)	114 ft 10 in (35 m)	114 ft 10 in (35 m)	114 ft 10 in (35 m)	107 ft 10 in (32.87 m)	114 ft 10 in (35 m)
Length	93 ft (28.35 m)	96 ft (29.26 m)	111 ft 6 in (33.99 m)	111 ft 6 in (33.99 m)	118 ft (35.97 m)	118 ft (35.97 m)
Wing area	2,015 sq ft (187.19 m²)	2,027 sq ft (188.31 m²)	2,121 sq ft (197.04 m²)	2,121 sq ft (197.04 m²)	2,059 sq ft (191.28 m²)	2,121 sq ft (197.04 m²)
Weight empty	46,300 lb (21,002 kg)	54,709 lb (24,816 kg)	69,710 lb (31,615 kg)	72,934 lb (33,083 kg)	73,816 lb (33,483 kg)	75,085 lb (34,059 kg)
Maximum take-off	105,000 lb (47,638 kg)	127,600 lb (57,879 kg)	145,000 lb (65,772 kg)	162,000 lb (73,493 kg)	162,000 lb (73,493 kg)	162,000 lb (73,493 kg)
Fuel capacity	6,050 Imp. gal. (27,503 lit)	6,907 Imp. gal. (31,395 lit)	8,359 Imp. gal. (38,000 lit)	8,908 Imp. gal. (40,495 lit)	7,800 Imp. gal. (35,460 lit)	8,908 Imp. gal. (40,495 lit)
Passenger seating	36	44 aft facing	78	74–106	101–119	<119
Maximum cruising speed	450 mph (725 km/h)	480 mph (772 km/h)	500 mph (805 km/h)	526 mph (846 km/h)	532 mph (856 km/h)	500 mph (805 km/h)
Range (max. pay load)	1,750 miles (2,816 km)	2,500 miles (4,023 km)	2,500 miles (4,023 km)	2,720 miles (4,380 km)	2,500 miles (4,823 km)	2,800 miles (4,506 km)
Cruising altitude	35,000 ft	40,000 ft	40,000 ft	42,000 ft	23,500 ft	33,000 ft
Take-off field length	5,350 ft	6,600 ft	6,500 ft	6,750 ft	6,750 ft	6,750 ft

	Nimrod Mr.1	Nimrod Mr.2	Nimrod R.1	Nimrod AEW.3	Nimrod MRA.4
Engines (4)	R-R Spey Mk 250	R-R Spey Mk 250	R-R Spey Mk 251	R-R Spey Mk 251	R-R BR 700-710-48M
Take-off thrust	12,500 lb (5,670 kg)	12,500 lb (5,670 kg)	12,500 lb (5,670 kg)	12,500 lb (5,670 kg)	15,577 lb (7,066 kg)
Span	114 ft 10 in (35 m)	114 ft 10 in (35 m)	115 ft 1 in (35.08 m)	115 ft 1 in (35.08 m)	127 ft (38.7 m)
Length	126 ft 9 in (38.63 m)	129 ft 1 in (39.34 m)	119 ft 9 in (36.5 m)	137 ft 8 in (41.97 m)	126 ft 9 in (38.63 m)
Wing area	2,121 sq ft (197.04 m²)	2,121 sq ft (197.04 m²)	2,121 sq ft (197.04 m²)	2,121 sq ft (197.04 m²)	2,538 sq ft (235.78 m²)
Weight empty	86,000 lb (39,010 kg)	92,000 lb (41,730 kg)	c 92,000 lb (41,730 kg)	c 88,000 lb (39,917 kg)	128,500 lb (58,288 kg)
Maximum take-off	177,500 lb (80,514 kg)	192,000 lb (87,090 kg)	177,500 lb (80,514 kg)	187,000 lb (84,823 kg)	232,315 lb (105,378 kg)
Fuel capacity	10,730 Imp. gal. (48,779 lit)	10,730 Imp. gal. (48,779 lit)	10,730 Imp. gal. (48,779 lit)	10,730 Imp. gal. (48,779 lit)	13,540 Imp. gal. (61,561 lit)
Endurance	12–15 h	12–15 h	15 h	15 h	16+ h
Range	5,758 miles (9,266 km)	5,758 miles (9,266 km)	5,758 miles (9,266 km)	c 5,000 miles (8,000 km)	7,000 miles (11,265 km)
Accomodation	3+9 (45/55 troops)	3+10 (45 troops)	3+28	4+6	2+8/10
External hardpoints	0 or 2	2	—	—	4

Index